The WordPerfect Tutorial

About the author   Joel Murach, a former assistant editor of *Strings* and *Acoustic Guitar* magazines, is a new staff writer for Mike Murach and Associates. He brings a working knowledge of *WordPerfect* features from his editing job to this tutorial.

Joel attended the University of California, Berkeley, and graduated in 1990 with a BA in music. He presently resides in the East Bay area.

The WordPerfect Tutorial

for DOS

Mike Murach & Associates

4697 West Jacquelyn Avenue, Fresno, California 93722
(209) 275-3335

Production team

Editor
Cris Allen

Graphics designer
Steve Ehlers

10 9 8 7 6 5 4 3 2 1

ISBN: 0-911625-77-1

Contents

Preface for instructors

This book is designed for a short course in *WordPerfect* 5.0 or 5.1. It consists of three instructional units that contain text as well as guided exercises for practice on a PC. These units are designed to teach a student how to use *WordPerfect* at a professional level of competence. To make it easy for an instructor to use this book, we offer an *Instructor's Guide* that provides complete supporting materials for classroom instruction including transparency masters, tests, and additional exercises and projects for practice on a PC.

We've tested the tutorial in this book on students with several levels of PC experience (including no experience at all), and we believe this is the most efficient *WordPerfect* tutorial currently available. Although some tutorials take less time, they don't teach the students what they need to know to be competent *WordPerfect* users. Worse, many tutorials take more time and still don't teach the students enough to be competent *WordPerfect* users. When your students finish this course, though, they are likely to discover that they're more competent than people who have been using *WordPerfect* for years.

To be competent *WordPerfect* users, of course, students need to know more than how to use the *WordPerfect* keystrokes and commands. Because *WordPerfect* often provides two or more methods for performing the same function, the students also need to know *when* to use the various keystrokes and commands. That's why the tutorial in this book takes the extra time to give a professional perspective on the use of *WordPerfect*. We think of that as teaching both keystrokes and concepts.

To make it possible to teach both keystrokes and concepts, each unit in the tutorial is divided into two main parts: text and exercises. When students read the text, they not only learn the keystrokes for using *WordPerfect*, they also get the perspective they need for using *WordPerfect* productively. Because the text is heavily illustrated, they can read and understand this portion of each unit without ever turning their PCs on. As a result, they can read the text before or after a classroom session.

Obviously, though, a student can't master *WordPerfect* just by reading about it. That's why the exercises for each unit are carefully designed to force the students to use all of the commands and functions presented in the text. With help from an instructor, the students can do the exercises for a unit before they read the text. But if they read the text before class, they can do the exercises more quickly so the instructor can go on to other subjects, exercises, and projects.

Which way works better? That depends on the instructor, the students, the lab environment, the number of class periods, and so on. If the students read the text before class, their questions will be more probing and they'll be able to do the exercises more quickly. If they read the text after class, it will improve their perspective and help them retain what they've learned. But either way, both the text and the exercises are an essential part of the learning process.

To support the tutorial in section 1 of this book, section 2 contains independent resource modules that the students can read whenever they need them. These modules are particularly useful if your students have limited PC experience. If, for example, your students don't know how to give a complete DOS specification for a *WordPerfect* file, module A shows them how to do that. And if they're having trouble with the concept of retrieving or saving files because they don't know the difference between hard disk storage and internal memory, module B gives them the hardware background that they need. As the instructor, you can direct your students to these modules when you discover that your students need these additional resources.

The last module in this resource section, module D, is a quick summary of the *WordPerfect* keystrokes and commands in the tutorial. This makes it easy for your students to find what they're looking for when they need to refresh their memory. Because the summaries and illustrations in the tutorial are the best reference materials that we know of, module D directs the students back to the figures that explain the functions that they're looking up. Normally, when students use the figures for reference, they don't even have to read the related text because the figures tell them all they need to know. That's why your students will appreciate this book long after the course is over.

As I said at the start of this preface, we offer an *Instructor's Guide* that provides a full set of supporting materials for this tutorial. It includes a complete set of transparency masters with presenter notes, short-answer tests, and additional exercises and projects. Although you can use these instructional materials for a course without using our books, we're convinced that this book will improve the effectiveness of any *WordPerfect* course. That's why we offer the *Instructor's Guide* free with any class-size order of books. Otherwise, the *Instructor's Guide* costs $150.

If you have any comments, criticisms, or suggestions, I would appreciate hearing from you. For your convenience, a comment form is included near the back of this book. And thanks for your interest in our books.

Mike Murach, Publisher
Fresno, California
January, 1993

Section 1

The tutorial

This section contains a tutorial that is designed to teach you *WordPerfect* at a professional level of competence as quickly as possible. To be a competent user, though, you need to know more than how to use the *WordPerfect* keystrokes and commands. Because *WordPerfect* often provides two or more methods for performing the same function, you also need to know *when* to use the various keystrokes and commands. That's why the tutorial in this book takes the extra time to give you a professional perspective on the use of *WordPerfect*.

To make it possible to teach both keystrokes and concepts, each unit in the tutorial is divided into two main parts: text and exercises. When you read the text, you not only learn the keystrokes that you need for using *WordPerfect*, but you also get the perspective you need for using it productively. Because the text is heavily illustrated, you can read and understand this portion of each unit without ever turning your PC on. Then, to help you master *WordPerfect*, the exercises for each unit force you to use all of the commands and functions presented in the text on a PC.

When you use this book as part of a course, your instructor will tell you whether you should read the text for a unit before or after you do the exercises. But either way, both the text and the exercises are an essential part of the learning process. You can't get the perspective you need without reading the text; and you can't get the guided practice that you need without doing the exercises.

How to create, print, and save a one-page letter

WordPerfect is a complex program that provides hundreds of commands and features. To learn how to use all of them takes many hours. Fortunately, you only need to know how to use a few *WordPerfect* commands and features to create, print, and save a letter. And that's what this unit is designed to teach you.

As you read this unit, you can try the skills it teaches on your own PC right after you read about them. If you use the unit in this way, you'll actually create a simple document like the one in figure 1-1 by the time you complete this unit. Or, you can read the entire unit first and then try the *WordPerfect* skills it teaches. Because the unit is heavily illustrated, you shouldn't have any trouble following this unit even if you don't have *WordPerfect* running on a PC in front of you. Then, you can go through the guided exercises at the end of the unit.

How to start *WordPerfect*

How you start *WordPerfect* depends on how your PC is set up. If your PC displays a menu or a shell program when you start it up, you can probably start *WordPerfect* by selecting an option from a menu. If your PC displays the DOS command prompt, you may be able to start *WordPerfect* by entering a batch file command like *wp* at the command prompt:

```
c:\>wp
```

If that doesn't work, you can start *WordPerfect* 5.1 by entering a series of commands like this at the command prompt:

```
D:\>c:
C:\>cd \wp51
C:\WP51>wp
```

To start *WordPerfect* 5.0, you substitute WP50 for WP51 in the series of commands above.

How to interpret the Edit screen

When you start *WordPerfect* 5.0, it displays a blank Edit screen like the top one in figure 1-2. If you're using *WordPerfect* 5.1, however, the program may be set up so it starts with either one of the Edit screens shown in figure 1-2. As you can see, the bottom screen has a bar at the top called the *menu bar*. If your PC displays a screen with the menu bar on it, just ignore the bar for now. It doesn't affect the way *WordPerfect* 5.1 works, and I'll show you how to use it later in this unit.

Figure 1-3 shows the Edit screen after the document that is printed in figure 1-1 has been entered into *WordPerfect*. The term *document* is used to refer to whatever you're working on when you use *WordPerfect*. For instance, letters, memos, reports, and proposals are all documents. In figure 1-3, the document is a letter. Although the entire document isn't shown because the screen can hold only 24 lines of the document, the entire document is stored in the internal memory of the PC.

Figure 1-3 also gives the terms that you need to know when you refer to the Edit screen. Here, you can see that the *cursor* is in the middle of the screen right after the colon. The cursor is the blinking underline or the highlight that identifies a specific character or area of a screen.

The *status line* is the bottom line of the screen. If you've saved your document, the left side of the status line shows the file specification for the document. Otherwise, this area is blank. The notation on the right side of the status line gives you the location of the cursor. In figure 1-3, for example, the *document indicator* shows that the cursor is in document 1 (*WordPerfect* lets you work on two different documents at the same time). The *page indicator* shows that the cursor is on page 1 of the document. The *line indicator* shows that the cursor is on the 14th line below the top margin. And the *position indicator* shows that the cursor is 34 characters from the left margin.

In figure 1-3, the cursor location is given in lines and characters. However, your system may be set up so that *WordPerfect* gives the location in inches as in this example:

Doc 1 Pg 1 Ln 1.33" Pos 3.58"

Here, the cursor is 1.33 inches below the top margin and 3.58 inches in from the left margin. But don't be bothered if your Edit screen looks different than the one in figure 1-3 because the differences don't affect the way that *WordPerfect* works.

How to use the keyboard with *WordPerfect*

Figure 1-4 shows the two most common kinds of keyboards in use today: the 84-key keyboard and the 101-key keyboard. If you study these keyboards, you can see that they have several types of keys including a full set of typewriter

```
                             August 20, 1992

Tim McCrystle
107 Merring Ct.
Sacramento, CA  95864

Dear Tim:

     Thanks for asking about our PC books.  I've enclosed a catalog
that describes them all in detail.  As you read through it, I hope
you'll find something you can use right away.

     So there's no risk to you, all our books are backed by our
unconditional guarantee:

     If our PC books aren't the best ones you've ever used for
     both training and reference, you can return them for a
     full refund.  No questions asked.

     If you have any questions or if you're ready to place an
order, please call us at our toll-free number: 1-800-221-5528.  And
thanks for your interest in our books.

                             Sincerely,



                             Karen DeMartin
```

Figure 1-1   A letter that was created and printed using *WordPerfect*

**The Edit screen
without the menu bar**

Doc 1 Pg 1 Ln 1 Pos 15

**The Edit screen with
the menu bar**

File Edit Search Layout Mark Tools Font Graphics Help

Doc 1 Pg 1 Ln 1 Pos 15

Figure 1-2   The starting screen for *WordPerfect* with and without the menu bar

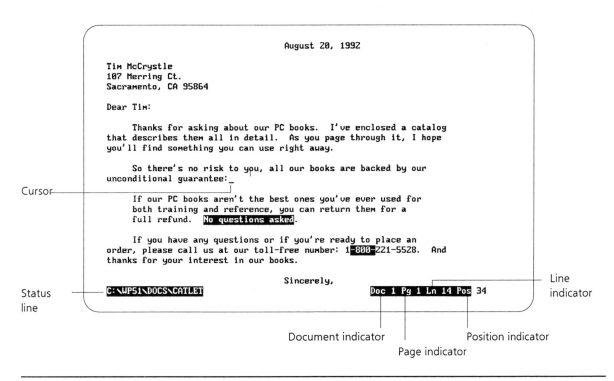

August 20, 1992

Tim McCrystle
107 Merring Ct.
Sacramento, CA 95864

Dear Tim:

Thanks for asking about our PC books. I've enclosed a catalog
that describes them all in detail. As you page through it, I hope
you'll find something you can use right away.

So there's no risk to you, all our books are backed by our
unconditional guarantee:

Cursor

If our PC books aren't the best ones you've ever used for
both training and reference, you can return them for a
full refund. No questions asked.

If you have any questions or if you're ready to place an
order, please call us at our toll-free number: 1-800-221-5528. And
thanks for your interest in our books.

Sincerely,

Line indicator

Status line

C:\WP51\DOCS\CATLET   Doc 1 Pg 1 Ln 14 Pos 34

Document indicator   Position indicator

Page indicator

Figure 1-3   The terms that apply to the Edit screen

keys, a set of numeric keys like the ten keys on a calculator, and some control
and function keys.

When you use the typewriter keys, most of them work just as they would
if you were using a typewriter. You can use these keys to type lower- and
uppercase letters, numbers, punctuation marks, and some special symbols.
When you hold down the Shift key, you get capital (uppercase) letters when
you press the letter keys, and you get the upper symbol of the two symbols on
the key when you press one of the other typewriter keys.

Figure 1-5 summarizes the use of the control keys that you will use most
often with *WordPerfect*. When you press the Caps-lock key, the keyboard is put
in Caps-lock mode. In this mode, the Caps-lock light is on, and the characters
Pos in the status line are changed to *POS*. Then, all the letter keys that you
strike will be entered into *WordPerfect* as capitals. However, the other keys on
the keyboard are not affected by this mode. To get the upper symbol on a
key, you must still hold down the Shift key while you press the key that you
want. To get out of Caps-lock mode, you just press the Caps-lock key again.
When a key switches between two or more modes like this, it is called a *toggle
key*.

The Tab key is used to indent text like the first line of a paragraph. And the Enter key is used to end a paragraph. As you will see in a moment, you don't need to use the Enter key at the end of each line as you do the Return key when you use a typewriter; you only need to use the Enter key to mark the end of a paragraph. Later, you'll learn that you also use the Enter key to end an entry that's required by *WordPerfect*.

The Backspace and Delete keys are used to delete text. If you press the Backspace key once, *WordPerfect* deletes the character to the left of the cursor. If you press the Delete key once, *WordPerfect* deletes the character at the cursor. If you hold down the Backspace key, *WordPerfect* deletes the character to the left of the cursor and continues deleting in that direction until you release the key or run out of text. If you hold down the Delete key, *WordPerfect* deletes the character at the cursor and continues to delete characters to the right until you release the key or run out of text.

The Arrow keys are sometimes called the *cursor control keys* because they are used to move the cursor through the text in a document. If you press the Right arrow key once, for example, *WordPerfect* moves the cursor one character to the right. If you press the Down arrow key once, *WordPerfect* moves the cursor down one line. And if you hold down any Arrow key, the cursor will continue to move in the direction of the arrow until you release the key. However, the Arrow keys can only be used to move through the existing text. So if you try to move the cursor to an area of the screen that doesn't have any text, *WordPerfect* won't move the cursor.

If you have an 84-key keyboard on your PC like the one shown in figure 1-4, you have to know how the Num-lock key affects the Arrow keys. Within the ten-key numeric pad of that keyboard, every key but the 5-key has a control function. For example, the 6-key is also the Right arrow key, and the 2-key is also the Down arrow key. To access the Arrow keys, you have to turn the Num-lock mode off. To turn this mode off if it's on, you press the Num-lock key. When the mode is off, the Num-lock light is off, and the characters *Pos* in the position indicator of the status line aren't blinking. Since you will use the Arrow keys frequently when you use *WordPerfect*, you will probably want to leave this mode off.

If you are using a 101-key keyboard, on the other hand, you will probably want to leave the Num-lock mode on. On this keyboard, the control keys are duplicated between the typewriter keys and the numeric pad. Then, if you keep the Num-lock mode on, you can use the control pad for control functions and the numeric pad for numeric entries.

The Insert key is used to toggle between *insert mode* and *typeover mode*. These two editing modes affect how text is inserted into your document. When you start *WordPerfect*, it is in insert mode, and this is the mode you'll use most of the time. In insert mode, the text that you type is inserted into the text by pushing the existing characters to the right.

**The 84-key
keyboard**

Note that the control keys and the numeric keys are combined in a single pad to the right of the typewriter keyboard. To use the numeric keys in the numeric pad, Numeric Lock (Num-lock) must be on. To use the control keys in the numeric pad, Numeric Lock must be off.

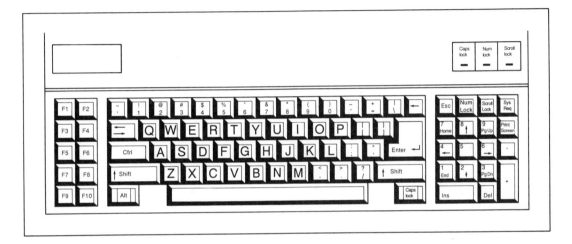

**The 101-key
keyboard**

Note that a separate set of control keys are located between the typewriter keys and the numeric pad. But the numeric pad still includes a second set of control keys. As a result, you still have to turn Numeric Lock (Num-lock) on if you want to enter numbers with the numeric pad. If you keep it on, you can use the control key pad for all control operations and the numeric pad for all data entry.

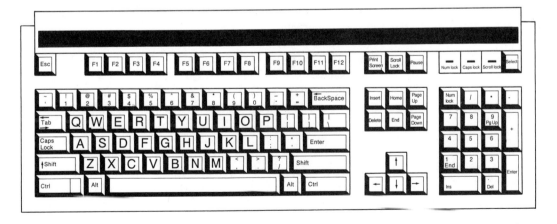

Figure 1-4   The 84-key and 101-key keyboards

Key	Function
Caps-lock	Turns Caps-lock mode on and off. If Caps-lock is on, the Caps-lock light is on, and the position indicator in the status line is displayed in capital letters (POS). Then, all the letter keys you strike appear as capital letters.
Tab	Indents the first line of a paragraph.
Enter	Ends a paragraph or ends an entry that is required by *WordPerfect*.
Backspace	Deletes the character to the left of the cursor.
Delete	Deletes the character at the cursor.
Arrow keys	Moves the cursor one character to the right or left, or moves the cursor one line up or down.
Num-lock	Turns Num-lock mode on and off. If Num-lock is on, the Num-lock light is on, and the position indicator (Pos) in the status line blinks. Then, when you use the numeric key pad, you get the number that's assigned to the key instead of the cursor control function that's assigned to the key.
Insert	Switches between Typeover and Insert modes. If Typeover mode is on, the word *Typeover* appears on the left side of the status line. Then, the characters you type overwrite the characters at the cursor. If Insert mode is on, the characters you type are inserted at the cursor.

Figure 1-5   Control keys that affect *WordPerfect* operations

When you press the Insert key, you switch to *typeover mode.* In this mode, your Edit screen displays the word *Typeover* on the left side of the status line at the bottom of the screen. Then, the text that you type will overwrite and replace the existing characters.

Once you understand how the Arrow keys and the two text editing modes work, you should be able to correct mistakes anywhere in your document. Just use the Arrow keys to move the cursor to where you want to start editing. Then, use the Delete key or the Backspace key to delete any characters you don't want. Next, use insert or typeover mode to type new characters into the document.

In the next unit, you'll learn how to use other keystrokes to move the cursor around your document more efficiently. And you'll learn how to delete text more efficiently. But for now, the Arrow keys, the Backspace key, and the Delete key are the only keys you need to know how to use.

How to enter the first portion of the letter into *WordPerfect*

If you're creating the letter shown in figure 1-1 as you read this unit, take the time now to enter the keystrokes as shown in figure 1-6. This figure shows all

```
[Tab][Tab][Tab][Tab][Tab]August 20, 1992[Enter]
[Enter]
Tim McCrystle[Enter]
107 Merring Ct.[Enter]
Sacramento, CA 95864[Enter]
[Enter]
Dear Tim:[Enter]
[Enter]
[Tab]Thanks for asking about our PC books. I've enclosed a catalog that describes them all in
detail. As you read through it, I hope you'll find something you can use right away.[Enter]
[Enter]
[Tab]So there's no risk to you, all our books are backed by our unconditional guarantee:[Enter]
[Enter]
```

Figure 1-6   The keystrokes for the first portion of the letter in figure 1-1

of the keystrokes required to enter the first portion of the letter. To start, press the Tab key several times so the date is located just past the center of the page. Although figure 1-6 shows that the key should be pressed five times, this depends on how *WordPerfect* has been set up on your PC. Later on, when you enter the signature block for the letter, you should use the same number of tabs that you used before the date.

After you type the date, press the Enter key to move the cursor to the next line. Then, press the Enter key again to skip a line. From this point on, type the keystrokes shown in figure 1-6 to finish the first portion of the letter. When you finish, your screen should look something like the one in figure 1-7. However, it won't look exactly the same unless your margins, tabs, and base font are set the same way they are for this example. I'll show you how to control those settings in unit 3.

When you type the first paragraph of the letter, you'll notice that you don't have to press the Enter key at the end of each line. Instead, *WordPerfect* automatically moves from the end of one line to the start of the next line. This is called *word wrap*. As a result, you only press the Enter key when you want to end a paragraph.

How to access and cancel *WordPerfect* commands

To enter the second portion of the letter in figure 1-1, you need to know how to use *WordPerfect* commands. Specifically, you need to know how to use the commands for indenting, underlining, and boldfacing. Also, when you complete the letter, you will need to know how to use the commands for printing the letter, saving the letter on the hard disk, and exiting from *WordPerfect*.

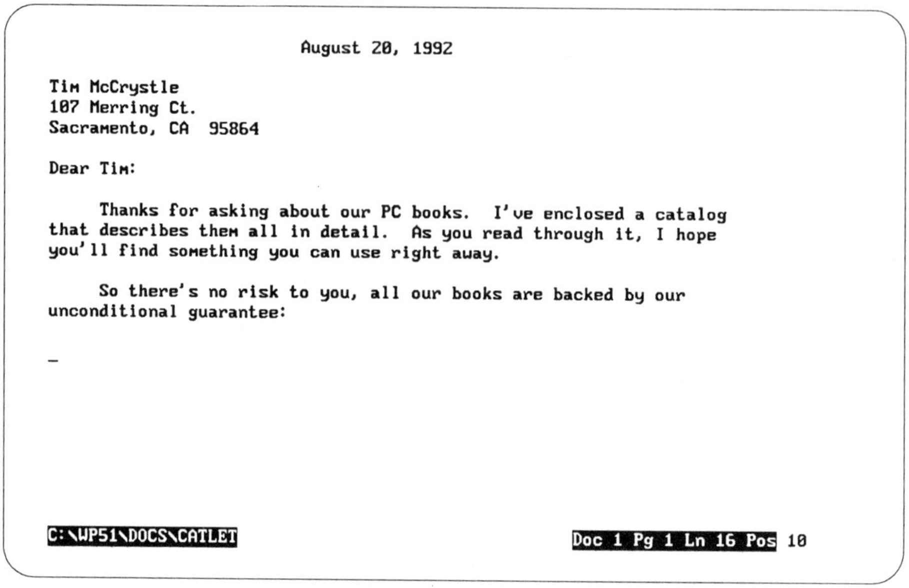

```
                          August 20, 1992

     Tim McCrystle
     107 Merring Ct.
     Sacramento, CA  95864

     Dear Tim:

          Thanks for asking about our PC books.  I've enclosed a catalog
     that describes them all in detail.  As you read through it, I hope
     you'll find something you can use right away.

          So there's no risk to you, all our books are backed by our
     unconditional guarantee:


     ―


     C:\WP51\DOCS\CATLET                          Doc 1 Pg 1 Ln 16 Pos 10
```

Figure 1-7   The Edit screen after the keystrokes in figure 1-6 have been entered into *WordPerfect*

To access commands when you're using *WordPerfect* 5.0, you use the function keys in combination with the Shift, Alt, and Ctrl keys. To access commands when you're using *WordPerfect* 5.1, you can use the function keys just as you do with release 5.0, or you can use the *WordPerfect* 5.1 menus. I'll show you how to access the commands using both methods, but you can skip the topic on the use of the menus if you're using release 5.0.

How to use the function keys to access the commands   If you look at figure 1-4 again, you'll see that both keyboards include ten function keys numbered from F1 through F10, and the 101-key keyboard includes two additional function keys numbered F11 and F12. Both keyboards include special control keys such as the Ctrl key, the Alt key, and the Shift key. By using the function and control keys in various combinations, you can access any one of the *WordPerfect* commands. To start the Print command, for example, you hold down the Shift key while you press the F7 key (Shift+F7).

A *WordPerfect template* is a piece of cardboard or plastic that summarizes how to access *WordPerfect* commands. The templates for the two types of keyboards are shown in figure 1-8. For the 101-key keyboard, the template lays across the top of the 12 function keys. For the 84-key keyboard, the template fits around the ten function keys. Although there are some minor differences between the templates for *WordPerfect* 5.0 and 5.1, these differences don't affect the commands presented in this book.

Figure 1-9 shows you how to use the Ctrl, Alt, and Shift keys to access the commands on just one of the function keys, the F4 key, but the concept is the same for all of the commands. To access the >Indent command (Single Indent command), you just press the function key. To access the >Indent< command (Double Indent command), you press the function key while holding down the Shift key. To access the Block command, you press the function key while holding down the Alt key. And to access the Move command, you press the function key while holding down the Ctrl key.

Because the first ten function keys have four commands each, you can use the command keys to access 40 commands. As you can see in the 101-key template in figure 1-8, the F11 and F12 keys don't provide for additional commands. Instead, they just make it easier to access the Reveal Codes and the Block commands, which can otherwise be accessed using the Alt+F3 and Alt+F4 key combinations.

To enter the second portion of the letter in figure 1-1, you need to access the >Indent< command, the Underline command, and the Bold command. If you look at the templates in figure 1-8, you can see that you access the >Indent< command using the Shift+F4 key combination. To access the Underline command, you press the F8 key by itself. Similarly, to access the Bold command, you press the F6 key by itself. In a moment, I'll explain how these commands work in more detail. But first, I want to show you how to access these commands using the *WordPerfect* 5.1. menu system.

How to use the *WordPerfect* 5.1 menus to access the commands

If you're using *WordPerfect* 5.1, you can use the function keys to access the commands just as you do with *WordPerfect* 5.0. However, you can also access the commands using the 5.1 menus. The menus don't provide new commands; they just provide another way to access the commands.

If you look at figure 1-10, you can see the elements that make up the menu system. At the top of the screen is the *menu bar* with nine menus on it. Since you pull these menus down when you want to use them, they are called *pull-down* menus. In the two examples in figure 1-10, the Layout menu and the Font menu have been pulled down.

If you look closely at the items on the Layout menu, you will see that some of them have a triangle to their right. When you select an item with a triangle, *WordPerfect* gives you another menu with more items. Since this type of menu cascades off to the right of the pull-down menu, it's called a *cascading menu*. In figure 1-10, for example, the Align menu cascades off to the right of the Align item on the Layout menu, and the Appearance menu cascades off of the Font menu. In contrast, when you select an item that doesn't have a triangle, *WordPerfect* starts the command.

Figure 1-11 summarizes the procedures for using the menus with or without a mouse. First, if the menu bar isn't already displayed on your screen,

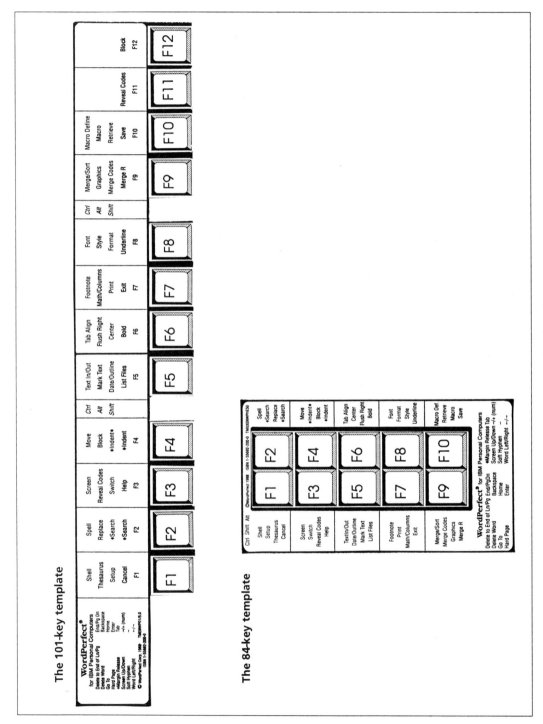

Figure 1-8 The *WordPerfect* command templates for the two styles of keyboards

Keystrokes	Command
Ctrl+F4	Move
Alt+F4	Block
Shift+F4	>Indent<
F4	>Indent

Figure 1-9 How to access the commands on the F4 function key

clicking the right mouse button will display the menu bar. Second, you move the mouse cursor to the menu you want to pull down, and you click the left mouse button. Third, you move the mouse cursor to the menu item you want and click the left mouse button. If this selection doesn't lead to a cascading menu, the command is started. Otherwise, you move the mouse cursor to the item that you want to select in the cascading menu and press the left mouse button to start that command. If you make a mistake or change your mind, you can cancel the command and return to the Edit screen by clicking the right mouse button.

If you're using the keyboard, you first transfer the cursor from the Edit screen to the menu bar by holding down the Alt key and pressing the Equals key (Alt+=). Or you may have to press just the Alt key, depending on how your PC is set up. This will also display the menu bar if it isn't already displayed. Second, you pull down the menu you want by pressing the highlighted letter of the menu. If, for example, you press the letter *l*, the Layout menu is pulled down. Third, you select an item from the menu by pressing the highlighted letter of the item. If this doesn't lead to a cascading menu, the command is started. Otherwise, you select an item from the cascading menu by pressing the highlighted letter of the item. Incidentally, you can also select a menu or a menu item by moving the cursor to it and pressing the Enter key. But that requires more keystrokes, so I don't recommend it. If you make a mistake or change your mind while you're accessing a command, you can press the Esc key or the Cancel key (F1) to return to the previous screen until you're back at the Edit screen. Or you can press the Exit key (F7) to return immediately to the Edit screen.

In general, I recommend that you avoid using the menu system because you can work more efficiently without it for three reasons. First, when you use the function keys to access commands, you can access any command with just one keystroke combination. In contrast, the menu system requires three or four keystrokes or clicks. Second, when you use the function keys to access commands, you don't have to remove your hands from the keyboard. In contrast, when you use a mouse, you have to switch one of your hands back

The two menus you use to select the >Indent< command

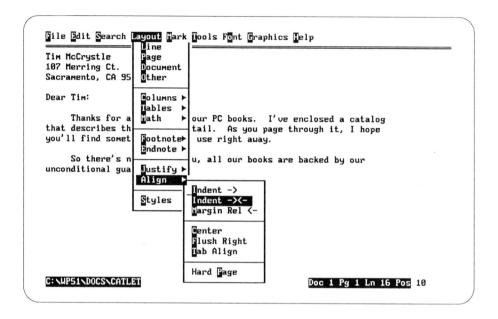

The two menus you use to select the Underline and the Bold commands

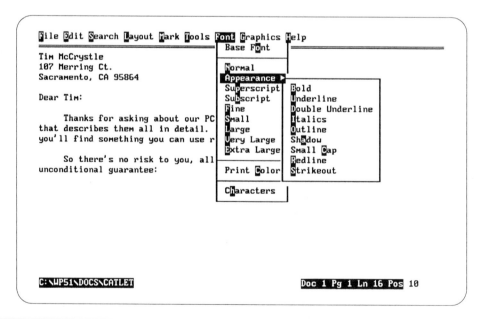

Figure 1-10   Two examples of the pull-down menus and cascading menus that you can use with *WordPerfect* 5.1

How to select commands using a mouse

1. If the menu bar isn't displayed at the top of the Edit screen, click the right mouse button.
2. To pull down a menu, move the mouse cursor to the menu you want and click the left mouse button.
3. To select a command, move the mouse cursor to the command you want and click the left mouse button.
4. If the command that you selected in step 3 leads to a cascading menu, move the mouse cursor to the command on that menu and select it by clicking the left mouse button.

How to select commands using the keyboard

1. If the menu bar isn't displayed at the top of the Edit screen, hold down the Alt key and press the Equals-sign key. On some PCs, all you have to do is press the Alt key to access the menu bar.
2. To pull down a menu, press the highlighted letter of the menu you want.
3. To select a command, press the highlighted letter in that command.
4. If the command that you selected in step 3 leads to a cascading menu, press the highlighted letter of the command on that menu to select it.

Figure 1-11   How to select commands from the *WordPerfect* 5.1 pull-down and cascading menus

and forth between the keyboard and mouse. Third, because mouse support and the menu system were added to *WordPerfect* in release 5.1, they aren't an integral part of the product. As a result, the menu interface doesn't work as efficiently or as logically as it ought to. Often, for example, you can't complete a command using the mouse and menu system alone so you end up using the keyboard anyway.

Since I recommend that you use the function keys instead of the menu system to access commands, I won't say any more about the use of menus or a mouse in this section of the book. Instead, I'll just show you how to use the function keys to access the commands. If you want to use the menu system, though, you can refer to module C. It covers the 5.1 menu system in detail.

How to use the Cancel command to cancel other commands   When you access commands like the Indent, Bold, and Underline commands, the command is started immediately. But when you access commands like the Move or Print commands, *WordPerfect* displays a screen or selection line that gives you options that you must choose from. Then, the command doesn't start until you complete your selections. In the meantime, if you decide that you don't want to perform the command after all, you can cancel it by pressing the Cancel key (F1).

[>Indent<]**If our PC books aren't the best ones you've used for both training and reference, you can return them for a full refund.** [Underline]**No questions asked**[Underline].[Enter]
[Enter]
[Tab]**If you have any questions or if you're ready to place an order, please call us at our toll-free number: 1**[Bold]**-800-**[Bold]**221-5528. And thanks for your interest in our books.**[Enter]
[Enter]
[Tab][Tab][Tab][Tab][Tab]**Sincerely,**[Enter]
[Enter]
[Enter]
[Enter]
[Tab][Tab][Tab][Tab][Tab]**Karen DeMartin**

Figure 1-12   The commands and keystrokes for the second portion of the letter in figure 1-1

You can also use the Esc key to cancel some commands, but this key won't work for all commands. At some of the screens that are displayed by commands, you can indicate that you don't want any of the options by pressing the Zero (0) key. This too has the effect of canceling a command. In the next unit, you'll learn more about these alternatives.

How to use the Indent, Underline, and Bold commands as you enter the second portion of the letter

If you're creating the letter shown in figure 1-1 as you read this unit, take the time now to enter the last portion of it. The commands and keystrokes that are required for this are shown in figure 1-12. In particular, there are three commands that are required to enter this portion of the letter.

To start, you access the Indent command. As you can see in figure 1-9, though, there are two different types of Indent commands. The first one (>Indent) indents only the left side of the paragraph. The second one (>Indent<) indents the left and the right sides of the paragraph, and that's the one you want to use in the letter. To access this command, you hold down the Shift key as you press the F4 key (Shift+F4). This starts the Double Indent command. From that point on, all the characters that you type will be indented from both sides until you press the Enter key.

The second command required in this letter is the Underline command. To access this command, you press the F8 key, which starts underlining immediately. To show that it has started, the number after the Position indicator on the status line is highlighted or changed to a different color. Then, when you type the text that you want to underline, *WordPerfect* colors or highlights it to indicate that it is underlined. Although this text usually isn't underlined on the Edit screen, it is underlined when you print it. To end the

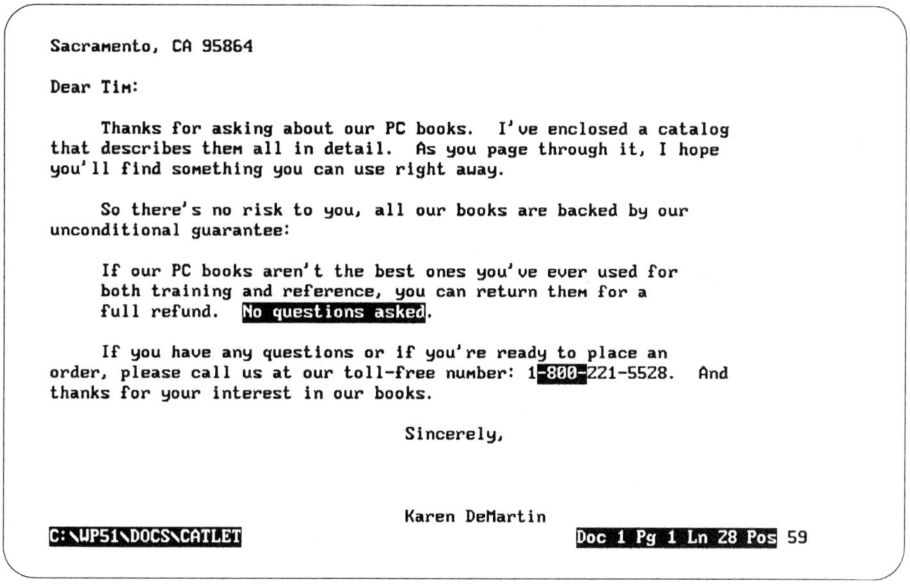

```
Sacramento, CA 95864

Dear Tim:

        Thanks for asking about our PC books.  I've enclosed a catalog
that describes them all in detail.  As you page through it, I hope
you'll find something you can use right away.

        So there's no risk to you, all our books are backed by our
unconditional guarantee:

        If our PC books aren't the best ones you've ever used for
        both training and reference, you can return them for a
        full refund.  No questions asked.

        If you have any questions or if you're ready to place an
order, please call us at our toll-free number: 1-800-221-5528.    And
thanks for your interest in our books.

                        Sincerely,




                        Karen DeMartin

C:\WP51\DOCS\CATLET                              Doc 1 Pg 1 Ln 28 Pos 59
```

Figure 1-13   The Edit screen after the letter in figure 1-1 has been entered into *WordPerfect*

Underline command, you can press F8 to access the command again, or you can press the Right arrow key.

As you enter the last paragraph of the letter, you need the Bold command. This command works like the Underline command. To access it, you press the F6 key. Then, you type the text that you want boldfaced. This text will be colored or highlighted on the screen to indicate that it is boldfaced, and it will be boldfaced when you print the document. To end the command, press F6 to access the command again or press the Right arrow key.

When you enter the signature block of the letter into *WordPerfect*, be sure to use the same number of Tabs that you used before the date. That way, the signature block will be aligned with the date.

As you type the signature block, the top of the letter will disappear, or *scroll off*, the top of the screen. In figure 1-13, for example, you can see that the date and the address have scrolled off the Edit screen. Then, if you want to look at the top of the letter, you can use the Up arrow key to scroll back up the letter.

How to use the Reveal Codes command

When you use *WordPerfect*, it inserts codes into your document. To keep the screen uncluttered, these codes are kept hidden from you. If you want to see these codes, though, you can do so by accessing the Reveal Codes command.

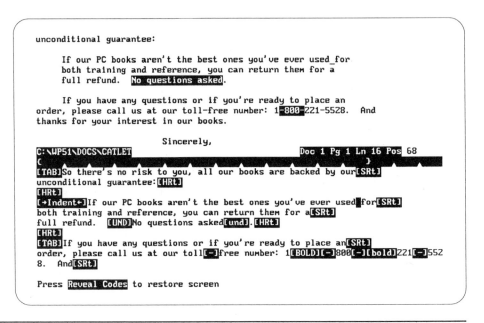

Figure 1-14   The Reveal Codes screen for the letter in figure 1-13

To access the Reveal Codes command, you hold down the Alt key as you press the F3 key (Alt+F3). This works on both the 84-key and the 101-key keyboard. If you have a 101-key keyboard, though, it's easier to access this command by pressing the Reveal Codes key (F11). To return to the Edit screen, just access the Reveal Codes command again.

After you access the Reveal Codes command, your screen will look like the one in figure 1-14. Here, the top half of the screen still looks like a normal Edit screen, but the bottom half of the screen shows both the text and the codes. In other words, the codes are revealed on the bottom half of the screen. In this figure, you can see that the status line is just above the line that separates the top and bottom halves of the screen. If you look closely, you can also see that the cursor is on both halves of the screen at the same time and in the same place (between the words *used* and *for*).

Figure 1-15 summarizes all the codes used in the letter in figure 1-14. As you see, *WordPerfect*'s word wrap function automatically inserts the *soft return* code [SRt] after each line in a paragraph. However, it inserts the *hard return* code [HRt] when you press the Enter key. Similarly, it inserts the Tab code [Tab] when you press the Tab key, and it inserts the Double Indent code [>Indent<] when you access the Double Indent command. Codes like these are referred to as a *single codes*.

In contrast, the Underline [UND][und] and Bold [BOLD][bold] codes are *paired codes*. The first code in the pair activates the command, and the second

Code	Name	Description
[SRt]	Soft Return	A single code that's automatically inserted at the end of each line. This code can't be deleted.
[HRt]	Hard Return	A single code that's inserted when you press the Enter key.
[Tab]	Tab	A single code that's inserted when you press the Tab key.
[>Indent<]	Double Indent	A single code that's inserted when you use the Double Indent command.
[UND][und]	Underline	A paired code that's inserted when you use the Underline command.
[BOLD][bold]	Bold	A paired code that's inserted when you use the Bold command.

Figure 1-15   A summary of the codes used in the completed letter

one turns it off. In figure 1-14, for example, you can see the Underline codes before and after this phrase: "No questions asked." Similarly, you can see the Bold codes before and after the -800- in the phone number.

When the Reveal Codes screen is displayed, it's easy to see why something in your document isn't working the way you want it to. Often, the problem is that the wrong code has been inserted into your document or that the right code is in the wrong place. Then, you can insert or delete the appropriate codes. As soon as you insert or delete a code, the change shows up in the formatting of the document.

To insert a single code, you move the cursor to the right location and press the key combination that inserts the code. Unfortunately, you can't insert a paired code as easily. To insert a paired code, you need to use an additional command called the Block command. I'll show you how to use that command in the next unit.

To delete a single code, you move the cursor to the code and press the Delete key. Similarly, to delete a paired code, you move the cursor to one of the codes in the pair and press the Delete key. Once you delete one code in a pair, both of the paired codes are deleted.

How to use the Print command

Figure 1-16 shows you how to use the Print command. To access this command, you hold down the Shift key as you press the F7 key (Shift+F7). When you do this, *WordPerfect* temporarily replaces the Edit screen with the Print screen. To begin printing, you select either the Full Document or Page option from the Print screen. You make your selection by typing either the

How to access the Print command

Hold down the Shift key and press the F7 key (Shift+F7).

The Print screen

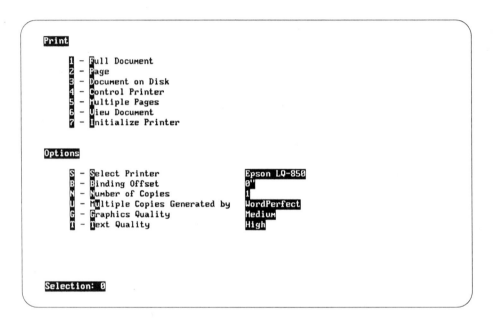

The primary Print options

The primary Print options	Meaning
1 or F	Print all of the pages in the document.
2 or P	Print only the page of the document that the cursor is on.

Figure 1-16   How to use the Print command to print a document

number of the option (1 or 2) or the highlighted letter in the option (F or P). Since the document in this unit is less than one page long, either of these options will print the entire document.

After you select Full Document or Page, *WordPerfect* starts the printing operation and returns you to your document. Then, you can continue working on the document while the printer prints. Or you can save your document and start working on another one. However, you can't exit from *WordPerfect* until it has finished the printing operation.

If your printer doesn't start printing after you start the printing operation, you should check to make sure that the printer is on, that the paper is loaded properly in the printer, and that the printer is ready for printing. As soon as the printer is ready, the *WordPerfect* document will start printing.

When your document is printed, you'll see that it doesn't look the same way that it does on the screen. In particular, the text that you underlined and boldfaced will be printed that way, even though they probably don't look that way on your screen. The paragraphs in your printed letter may be aligned at the right margin, even though they aren't aligned that way on the screen. And the text may appear in a typeface (or font) that's different from the typeface that appears on your screen. These differences are controlled by several *WordPerfect* settings, and in unit 3, I'll show you how to change those settings.

How to use the Save command

If you shut off your PC or exit from *WordPerfect* without saving your document, your work is lost. That's why you must understand what the Save command does and how it works. As you will see, this command works slightly differently for a new document than it does for an old one. This is summarized in figure 1-17.

How to save a document for the first time
The first procedure in figure 1-17 shows you how to use the Save command to save a document for the first time. In step 1, you press the F10 key to start the command. Then, *WordPerfect* displays a message, or *prompt*, that asks for the file specification that you want to use for the document:

Document to be saved:

If you enter just a file name, your document is saved in the *default directory*. If you enter a complete file specification, though, the directory in the specification is used instead of the default directory. After you enter the file specification, press the Enter key to complete the command.

In the next unit, you'll learn how to set the default directory to the one you want. But for now, just type the complete file specification when you use the Save command. If, for example, you want to save a file named CATLET on the D drive in the \DOCS directory, you enter a file specification like this:

Document to be saved: d:\docs\catlet

When you create a file name for a document, you must follow the DOS rules for file names. You should also try to create file names that you'll remember later on. In this example, I used CATLET to indicate that the file is a letter (LET) about a catalog (CAT). If you don't know the rules for creating file names or if you don't know how to enter a complete file specification, you should refer to module A.

If you try to save a document in a directory that doesn't exist, *WordPerfect* will flash a prompt like this:

ERROR: Invalid drive/path specification

Then, it will give you the Save prompt again with your invalid specification. To correct it, you can use the Arrow keys to move the cursor to the right location; you can use the Backspace and Delete keys to delete characters; and you can use the insert and typeover modes to insert or typeover characters. When you press the Enter key, *WordPerfect* will try to save the file again.

How to save a document for the second time   Suppose now that you want to change the address of the letter from 107 Merring Ct. to 4112 Redwood Road. Then, after you print the letter, you want to save the document so it will include this address change. The second procedure in figure 1-17 shows you how to do that.

After you access the Save command by pressing the F10 key, *WordPerfect* displays a prompt that gives the complete file specification that you used when you saved the file the first time. Then, since the specification is the way you want it, you don't have to enter it again. Instead, you just press the Enter key.

This time, however, there's already a file on the hard disk with the file name you've just used for the save operation. As a result, *WordPerfect* doesn't store the document on the disk right away. Instead, it displays a prompt that asks you whether you want to replace the old version of the document with the new one. Then, if that's what you want to do, type *y* for Yes. If that isn't what you want to do, type *n* for No so you can change the file specification. And if you decide that you don't want to save the file at all, press the Esc or F1 key to cancel the command.

How to save a revised document with a new name   Suppose now that you decide to make the letter you've been working on a form letter so you can use it repeatedly. To do that, delete the date, name and address, and the greeting from the letter, but leave in the tabs and blank lines. When you're done, your document will look like the one in figure 1-18. Then, after you print the letter, you want to save the document with a new name. The last procedure in figure 1-17 shows you how to do that.

After you access the Save command, *WordPerfect* displays a prompt that shows you the file specification that you used to save the file last time. This time, however, you want to change the file name, but not the path. To do that, use the Right arrow key to move to the file name portion of the specification. Then, delete or insert the required characters. In figure 1-17, the name is changed by adding the extension .FM to it (the period followed by the letters *FM*). If you use an extension, remember that it can't be more than three characters.

How to save a document for the first time

1. Press the F10 key to start the Save command. *WordPerfect* then displays this prompt that asks you to enter a file specification:

   `Document to be saved:`

2. Type the file specification for the file that you want created like this:

   `Document to be saved: c:\wp51\docs\catlet`

   Then, press the Enter key. This file specification is for a document to be named CATLET that will be stored in the \DOCS directory that's subordinate to the \WP51 directory on the C drive.

How to replace the document with a revised version of the document

1. Press the F10 key to start the Save command. *WordPerfect* then displays this prompt followed by the complete file specification for the document that you're working on:

   `Document to be saved: C:\WP51\DOCS\CATLET`

2. Press the Enter key to save the revised version of the document with the same file specification that you used before. Then, *WordPerfect* displays this prompt:

   `Replace C:\WP51\DOCS\CATLET? No (Yes)`

3. Press *y* for Yes to tell *WordPerfect* that you want to replace the old version of the document with the new version. *WordPerfect* then completes the command.

How to save a revised version of an old document under a new name

1. Press the F10 key to start the Save command. *WordPerfect* then displays this prompt followed by the complete file specification for the document that you're working on:

   `Document to be saved: C:\WP51\DOCS\CATLET`

2. Change the file specification to the one that you want to use for the revised version of the document like this:

   `Document to be saved: C:\WP51\DOCS\CATLET.fm`

   Then, press the Enter key. Here, the path remains the same, but the file name has been changed from CATLET to CATLET.FM. To make this change, you can use the Right arrow key to move to the end of the file specification before you type the period and the extension. (CATLET will remain unchanged and the revised version of the document will be saved under the name CATLET.FM.)

Figure 1-17   How to use the Save command to save a document to disk storage

```
   Dear :

        Thanks for asking about our PC books.  I've enclosed a catalog
   that describes them all in detail.  As you page through it, I hope
   you'll find something you can use right away.

        So there's no risk to you, all our books are backed by our
   unconditional guarantee:

        If our PC books aren't the best ones you've ever used for
        both training and reference, you can return them for a
        full refund.  No questions asked.

        If you have any questions or if you're ready to place an
   order, please call us at our toll-free number: 1-800-221-5528.   And
   thanks for your interest in our books.

                                    Sincerely,

   C:\WP51\DOCS\CATLET                                    Doc 1 Pg 1 Ln 7 Pos 15
```

Figure 1-18   The form letter created by revising the letter in figure 1-1

When you press the Enter key, the command is performed. Then, since the command uses a new file specification, the file is stored on the disk and *WordPerfect* returns to the Edit screen. In this example, that means that the old version of the file is still stored on the disk under the name CATLET, and the new version is stored under the name CATLET.FM.

How to use the Exit command

When you're through with the document you've been working on, you use the Exit command to exit from the document in one of two ways. First, you can use this command to exit from the document, but remain in *WordPerfect*. This will clear your Edit screen so you can start work on another document. Second, you can use this command to exit from *WordPerfect* and return to DOS or the program that you started *WordPerfect* from. Both of these options are summarized in figure 1-19.

The first procedure in figure 1-19 shows how to exit from a document, but not from *WordPerfect*. When you start the Exit command by pressing the F7 key, *WordPerfect* gives you a chance to save your document, but you should have already saved it. To make sure that you've saved your last modifications

How to exit from a document without saving it and without exiting from *WordPerfect*

1. Press the F7 key to start the Exit command. *WordPerfect* then displays this prompt that asks you if you want to save the document you've been working on:

   `Save document? Yes (No)                    (Text was not modified)`

   If you haven't made any changes to the document since the last time you saved it, you'll see a message on the right side of the prompt that says "Text was not modified."

2. Press *n* for No to indicate that you don't want to save the document you've been working on. *WordPerfect* then displays this prompt that asks you if you want to exit from the program:

   `Exit WP? No (Yes)`

3. Press *n* for No to indicate that you don't want to exit from *WordPerfect*. This clears the Edit screen so you can start work on another document.

How to exit from *WordPerfect* without saving the document you've been working on

1. Press the F7 key to start the Exit command. *WordPerfect* then displays this prompt that asks you if you want to save the document you've been working on:

   `Save document? Yes (No)                    (Text was not modified)`

   If you haven't made any changes to the document since the last time you saved it, you'll see a message on the right side of the prompt that says "Text was not modified."

2. Press *n* for No to indicate that you don't want to save the document you've been working on. *WordPerfect* then displays this prompt that asks you if you want to exit from the program:

   `Exit WP? No (Yes)`

3. Press *y* for Yes to indicate that you want to exit from *WordPerfect*.

Figure 1-19   How to use the Exit command to clear the Edit screen or to exit from *WordPerfect*

to the document, though, you can check the right side of the status line to see whether this message is displayed:

(Text was not modified)

If it is displayed, it means that you've already saved your last modifications to the document, so you can answer *n* for No at the first prompt. Then, *WordPerfect* displays a prompt that asks you whether you want to exit from *WordPerfect*. If you enter *n* for No, *WordPerfect* returns you to a blank Edit screen so you can start work on another document.

The second procedure in figure 1-19 shows you how to exit from *WordPerfect*. As in the first procedure, *WordPerfect* gives you another chance to save your document when you start the Exit command. Assuming that you've already saved your document, you enter *n* for No. Then, *WordPerfect* asks you whether you want to exit from the program and return to DOS. This time, you enter *y* for Yes to return to DOS.

Although you can use the Exit command to save a document before exiting from a document or *WordPerfect*, I recommend that you use the Save command before the Exit command. Then, you can answer No when the first prompt of the Exit command asks you whether you want to save the document you've been working on. Should you answer Yes, the prompts that follow work just like those for the Save command. Then, after you save the document, you can either exit from *WordPerfect* or just from the document.

Discussion

The hardest part about learning *WordPerfect* is getting started. Before you can do anything, you have to learn some basic terminology. You have to learn how to enter text. You have to understand how *WordPerfect* uses codes. And you have to learn how to use the *WordPerfect* commands.

If you've had any difficulty understanding the skills presented in this unit, I recommend that you do the exercises that follow on your own PC. They force you to use the skills in a more controlled manner than the text does. By the time you complete the exercises, you should be able to do all of the tasks presented in this unit. Then, you'll be ready for the next unit.

In the next unit, you'll learn skills that build upon the ones presented in this unit. For instance, you'll learn how to retrieve an old document from the hard disk; how to put the current date into a document without typing it; and how to use several other *WordPerfect* commands. After that, you'll be on your way to becoming a proficient *WordPerfect* user.

Terms

menu bar	word wrap
document	template
cursor	pull-down menu
status line	cascading menu
document indicator	scroll off
page indicator	soft return
line indicator	hard return
position indicator	single code
toggle key	paired code
cursor control key	prompt
insert mode	default directory
typeover mode	

Objectives

1. Enter text into *WordPerfect* using the typewriter keys including the Tab and Enter keys.

2. Make corrections to the text that you've entered by using the Arrow keys, the Backspace key, the Delete key, insert mode, and typeover mode.

3. Access any of the *WordPerfect* commands using the template and the function keys.

4. Use the eight commands presented in this unit to perform any of these functions:

   a) Double indent a portion of text.
   b) Underline a portion of text.
   c) Boldface a portion of text.
   d) Save a document.
   e) Print a document.
   f) Exit from a document and clear the screen.
   g) Exit from *WordPerfect*.
   h) Reveal the codes within a document.
   i) Cancel a command.

5. Use the Reveal Codes screen to locate and delete any of the single or paired codes in a document.

6. Insert single codes in a document after the document has been entered into *WordPerfect*.

Exercises

Part 1: How to enter text into *WordPerfect* and how to use some of the control keys

1. Start *WordPerfect*. Is the menu bar displayed on your Edit screen? Do the line and position indicators in the status line use inches or units? What is the location of the cursor before you enter any characters?

2. Press the Num-lock key to turn the Num-lock light on. When the light is on, the characters *Pos* in the status line blink. Next, use the numeric pad to enter some numbers. Then, press the Num-lock key again to turn the light off and try to use the numeric pad to enter more numbers. Note that *Pos* in the status line stops blinking when the Num-lock light is off. To delete the numbers that you entered, use the Backspace key to return to the first position of the document.

3. Use the typewriter keyboard to type these characters:

   abcdef123456-=[]\;',./<_>!@#$%^&*()_+{}|:"<>?

Note that you have to use the Shift key to type some of the characters.

Next, press the Caps-lock key to turn the Caps-lock light on. When you do this, note that the characters *Pos* in the status line are capitalized. Then, type the characters shown above again, but this time with capital instead of lowercase letters. Note that you still have to use the Shift key to type some of the characters.

To delete the characters that you've entered, use the Arrow keys to move the cursor to the first position in the document. Then, hold down the Delete key to delete all the characters that you entered. Next, press the Caps-lock key again to turn the Caps-lock feature off.

4. Type your name and address. After each line, press the Enter key to return the cursor to the left margin. Next, use the Arrow keys to move the cursor to the start of the second line of the document. Then, type the digits 1 through 9. Note how they are inserted into the line. Press the Insert key to change from insert to typeover mode, and enter the digits 1 through 9 again. Note how these digits replace the other characters in the line.

Hold down the Left arrow key and note the movement of the cursor. When it reaches the left margin, it continues backwards through the lines above it until it reaches the first position of the document and stops. Next, hold down the Right arrow key and note the movement of the cursor. It moves forward through the lines of the document until it reaches the last position in the document and stops.

5. Before you continue with the next set of exercises, you need to: (1) turn off typeover mode, and (2) return to a blank Edit screen. To turn off typeover mode, you press the Insert key; to return to a blank Edit screen, you press the F7 key for the Exit command. Then, when *WordPerfect* asks if you want to save the document, press *n* for No. And when *WordPerfect* asks if you want to exit from WP, press *n* for No. This erases what you've been working on and returns you to a blank screen.

Part 2: How to create, print, and save a letter

6. Type the first portion of the letter shown in figure 1-1 using the keystrokes in figure 1-6. If you prefer, use the current date instead of the date shown and use the name and address of a friend or relative. As you type the first and second paragraphs in the letter, note how the word wrap function works. When you finish, your screen should look similar to the one in figure 1-7. It won't look exactly the same unless your margins, tab settings, and base font happen to be the same as those used for this document.

7. Type the second portion of the letter shown in figure 1-1 using the keystrokes in figure 1-12. To start, look at the template on your keyboard and find the >Indent< command. To access this command, hold down the Shift key while you press the F4 key (Shift+F4) Then, type the first sentence in figure 1-12 followed by two spaces.

   The next sentence in figure 1-12 is supposed to be underlined. To do that, look at the template on your keyboard and find the Underline command. To access this command, just press the F8 key. Then, type "No questions asked," press the F8 key again to end underlining, press the Period key, and press the Enter key to end the double indentation.

   Continue by typing the next paragraph of figure 1-12. When you reach the part of the phone number to be boldfaced, find the Bold command on the template and press the F6 key to access it. Then, type "-800-," press the F6 key again to end the boldfacing, and continue.

   When you type the signature block of the letter, be sure to use the same number of tab characters that you used for indenting the date at the top of the letter. Also, use your own name instead of the name shown.

   When you've finished entering the letter, your Edit screen should look like the one in figure 1-13. Again, your margins and tab settings may not be exactly the same as the ones shown here. Note how your system shows that text has been underlined or boldfaced.

8. Find the Reveal Codes command on your template. If you have a 101-key keyboard you should find this command in two places. Then, start this command to display a Reveal Codes screen like the one in figure 1-14. On the lower half of this screen, find the codes for the Indent, Underline, and Bold commands. Also, find the codes for tabs, soft returns, and hard returns. You can do this by using the Up arrow key to move the cursor up through the document.

   Use the Arrow keys to move the cursor to one of the soft return codes [SRt]. Note that each half of the screen has its own cursor and that the cursors are in the same locations on both halves of the screen. Press the Delete key to delete the soft return code, and note that you can't delete it. Instead, the character or space to the left of the code is deleted. Replace this character or space by typing it again.

   Use the Arrow keys to move the cursor to the >Indent< code. Press the Delete key to delete it, and note the results. Then, access the command again to insert the code back into the letter. Finally, access the Reveal Codes command again to return to the normal Edit screen.

9. Use the template to find the Print command, and access it by holding down the Shift key while you press the F7 key (Shift+F7). This displays a screen like the one in figure 1-16. Next, press the F1 key to cancel this command.

Start the Print command again. This time, when the Print screen is displayed, press *1* or *f* to print the entire document. Note that you are returned to the Edit screen while the letter is being printed so you can continue your work.

10. Use the template to find the Save command, and access it by pressing the F10 key. This displays a prompt that asks you for the name of the document to be saved, but it doesn't tell you what the default directory is. Enter a complete file specification at this prompt including drive, directory, and file name (CATLET) so you'll know what directory the file is saved in. If you're saving your document to a diskette, you'll specify drive A or B. If you're saving your document to the hard drive, your instructor can tell you what drive and directory to use.

11. Use the Arrow keys to move the cursor to the first character in the first line of the address near the top of the letter. Next, press the Insert key to put the keyboard in typeover mode. Then, type a new address in this line and delete any leftover characters at the end of the line. You now have a revised version of the document you saved in the last exercise.

Access the Save command to save this revised version as shown in the second procedure of figure 1-17. This command displays a prompt that gives the complete file specification that you used when you saved the first version of the letter. To save it again with the same name, press the Enter key. *WordPerfect* then displays a prompt that asks you whether you want to replace the old file. Press *y* for Yes to complete the Save command.

Part 3: How to revise an old document and save it with a new name

12. Hold down the Up arrow key to move the cursor to the top of the letter. Next, access the Reveal Codes command to reveal the codes. Then, delete the date, the name and address, and the greeting at the top of the letter, as shown in figure 1-18, but don't delete the Tab [Tab] and Enter [HRt] codes. This revised letter will be used as the basis for a form letter. Last, access the Reveal Codes command again to return to the normal Edit screen.

13. Use the Print command to print this version of the letter. This time when the Print screen is displayed, press *2* or *p* to print the one-page letter.

14. Use the Save command to save this version of the letter under a new name as shown in the third procedure in figure 1-17. After you start this command, *WordPerfect* will display a prompt that shows the complete file specification that you used the last time you saved the letter. This time, though, change the file name, but not the drive or path. To do that, use

the Right arrow key to move to the end of the specification. Then, type a period followed by the letters *fm* to add an extension to the old filename. When you press the Enter key, the revised letter is saved under the new file specification. Now, there are two versions of this letter in your directory: one in the file named CATLET, and another in the file named CATLET.FM.

15. Use the template to find the Exit command. Then, press F7 to access this command. When the prompt asks whether you want to save the document you've been working on, press *n* for No (because you've just saved it). When the next prompt asks whether you want to exit from WP, press *n* for No to return to a blank Edit screen.

Access the Exit command again. This time press *n* to indicate that you don't want to save the document. Then, press *y* to indicate that you do want to exit from WP. This returns you either to the DOS prompt or to the program that you started *WordPerfect* from.

Unit 2

How to retrieve and edit the letter

In unit 1, you learned how to create, print, and save a one-page letter like the one shown in figure 2-1. Now, you'll learn how to retrieve and edit that letter. Along the way, you'll learn how to use seven more commands.

In word processing terms, when you *edit* a document, you make changes to it. That includes changes to words, paragraphs, and sentences like correcting misspellings, improving sentence clarity, adding new ideas, and deleting unnecessary ideas. But it also includes formatting changes like making the left and right margins of a document wider and centering a letter between the top and bottom margins.

As you read this unit, you can try the *WordPerfect* skills it teaches on your own PC right after you read about them. Or you can read the entire unit first and then go through the exercises at the end of the unit. When you do the exercises, you will modify the form letter shown in figure 2-1 so that it looks like the one in figure 2-17.

How to use the List command

The F5 key accesses a command called the List File command in *WordPerfect* 5.0 and the List command in *WordPerfect* 5.1. Since these commands are essentially the same, I'll refer to them both as the List command in this book.

You can use the List command for several different functions that are related to file handling. For instance, you can use it to change the default directory, to retrieve files, to copy files, to delete files, and so on. In this unit, I'll show you how to use this command for the first two of these functions, and I'll introduce you to some of its other functions too.

How to use the List command to set the default directory
One of the most important uses of the List command is changing the default directory. The *default directory* is the one that *WordPerfect* uses for saving and retrieving files when you don't specify the drive or directory in your file specifications. If, for example, you use the Save command to save a new file

with the name CATLET, the file is stored in the default directory. Often, though, the default directory isn't the one that you want your files stored in.

The first procedure in figure 2-2 shows you how to change the default directory. In step 1, you access the List command (F5). Then, *WordPerfect* displays a prompt like this:

Dir C:\WP51*.*   **(Type = to change default Dir)**

The first part of this prompt tells you the name of the current default directory. In this example, the default directory is C:\WP51. The second part of this prompt tells you to type the equals sign (=) if you want to change the default directory.

In step 2, you tell *WordPerfect* that you want to change the default directory by typing in the equals sign. Then, *WordPerfect* displays a prompt like this:

New Directory = C:\WP51

In step 3, you replace or modify the directory shown so it's the one that you want for your document files. To do that, you can just type the drive and directory specification that you want. Or if you prefer, you can use the Arrow keys, the Backspace and Delete keys, and the insert and typeover modes to modify the specification that's shown. When the drive and directory are correct, you press the Enter key.

At this point, the default directory has been changed, and *WordPerfect* displays a prompt that shows the new default directory. If, for example, you change the directory to the \WPDOCS directory on the D drive, the prompt looks like this:

Dir D:\WPDOCS*.*

In step 4, you can press the Enter key if you want to see a listing of the files in this directory, or you can press the Esc key or Cancel key (F1) if you want to return to the Edit screen. If you press the Enter key, *WordPerfect* displays a screen like one of the ones in figure 2-3.

How to use the List command to retrieve a file   The second
procedure in figure 2-2 shows you how to use the List command to retrieve a file. In step 1, you access the List command. Then, *WordPerfect* displays the prompt that shows the default directory. If this is the one that contains your document files, you press the Enter key to display the List screen.

If the default directory isn't the one that you want to list, you have two options. First, you can change the default directory by typing an equals sign and continuing as in the first procedure in figure 2-2. Then, when you press the Enter key, the new default directory is displayed. Second, you can modify the directory that is displayed in the prompt and press the Enter key. This displays the List screen for the directory that you specify, but it doesn't

```
Dear :

     Thanks for asking about our PC books.  I've enclosed a catalog
that describes them all in detail.  As you read through it, I hope
you'll find something you can use right away.

     So there's no risk to you, all our books are backed by our
unconditional guarantee:

     If our PC books aren't the best ones you've ever used for
     both training and reference, you can return them for a
     full refund.  No questions asked.

     If you have any questions or if you're ready to place an
order, please call us at our toll-free number: 1-800-221-5528. And
thanks for your interest in our books.

                    Sincerely,


                    Karen DeMartin
```

Figure 2-1　　The CATLET.FM form letter from unit 1

How to use the List command to change the default directory

1. Access the List command (F5) to display the prompt for the default directory:

   Dir C:\WP51*.*   (Type **= to change default Dir**)

2. When you type the equals sign (=), *WordPerfect* displays this prompt:

   New Directory = C:\WP51

3. Type the drive and directory that you want as the default directory as in this example:

   New Directory = d:\wpdocs

   Then, press the Enter key to change the directory and complete the command.

   Dir D:\WPDOCS*.*

4. If you want to see the List screen for the default directory, press the Enter key. If you want to return to the Edit screen, press the Esc or Cancel key. Either way, the new default directory is in effect for the current work session.

How to use the List command to retrieve a file

1. Access the List command (F5) to display the prompt for the default directory:

   Dir D:\WPDOCS*.*   (**Type =** to change default Dir)

2. If the file you want is in this directory, press the Enter key to display the List screen.

   If the file you want isn't in the default directory, you can continue in one of two ways. First, you can change the default directory as described above. Second, you can specify the directory you want by typing it in at the prompt. If you don't type the equals sign before you type in the directory specification, the default directory won't be affected. Then, when you have the directory you want, press the Enter key to display the List screen.

3. Use the Arrow keys to move the cursor on the List screen to the file you want to retrieve.

4. Use the Retrieve option to retrieve the file by pressing *1* or *r*.

Figure 2-2   How to use the List command to set the default directory and retrieve a file

change the default directory. When you exit from the List screen, the old default directory is still in effect.

Once a List screen like the one in figure 2-3 is displayed, it's easy to retrieve a file. Just use the Arrow keys to move the highlight to the file you want to retrieve. Then, press either *1* or *r* as indicated by the options at the bottom of the screen. If, for example, you want to retrieve the file named

CATLET.FM, you move the highlight to the second file listed in figure 2-3 and press *r*. *WordPerfect* then retrieves the file and returns you to the Edit screen.

Before you retrieve a file, you usually want to be sure that the Edit screen is empty. That means that you haven't entered any codes or characters into it and that you haven't retrieved another document into it. If you try to retrieve a document into an Edit screen that isn't empty (even one that contains just one space), *WordPerfect* displays a prompt like this one:

Retrieve into current document? No (Yes)

Although there are times when you want to retrieve one document into another document, you probably won't want to do that this early in your training. So you can press *n* for No. Then, after you use the Exit command to clear the screen, you can retrieve the file without getting this prompt.

How to use the List command for other functions   If you look at the options at the bottom of the screens in figure 2-3, you can see that you can use this screen to perform several functions. The second and third options, for example, let you Delete and Move (or rename) files. And the eighth option lets you Copy files. These options make it easy for you to manage files without using DOS.

The fourth option lets you Print a file on disk without retrieving it first. And the seventh option gives you another way to change the default directory. Normally, though, you just type the equals sign to change the directory when you first access the List command. So you won't use this option often.

The sixth option is the Look option. This option lets you display the document that's highlighted before you retrieve it. This option comes in handy when you're not sure that the document you highlighted is the one that you want to retrieve. To access the Look option, you press the Enter key because this option is the default option for the List command. You can tell that 6 is the default by looking at the number that appears at the end of the option selections. After you press the Enter key to look at a file and confirm that it's the right one, you press Enter or Exit to return to the List screen and *1* or *r* to retrieve the file.

If you compare the options in figure 2-3 for *WordPerfect* 5.0 and 5.1, you can see that there are some minor differences. In particular, the fifth options have different functions, and the ninth options have different words (but similar functions). You should be able to use most of the options for the List command just by experimenting with them. All you have to do is highlight the file you want to perform a function on, press the number or letter of the function that you want to perform, and do whatever the prompts ask for after that. To return to the Edit screen from the List screen without performing a function, you can press the Esc or Cancel key (F1); you can press the Exit key

The List screen for *WordPerfect* **5.1**

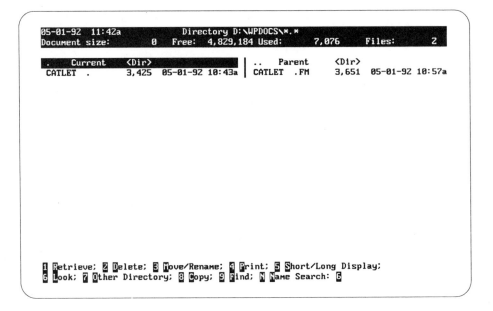

The List Files screen for *WordPerfect* **5.0**

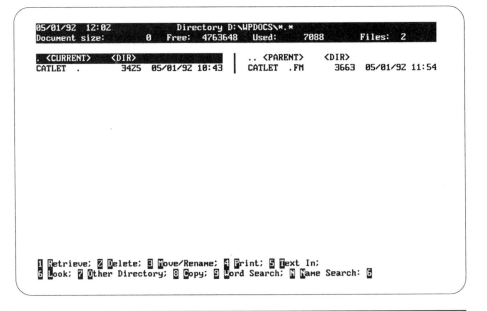

Figure 2-3   The List screens for releases 5.0 and 5.1

---

1. Access the Retrieve command (Shift+F10) to display this prompt:

   Document to be retrieved:

2. If the default directory is set to the one that contains the file you want, type the name of the file as in this example:

   Document to be retrieved: catlet

   Then, press the Enter key to complete the command.

Figure 2-4   How to use the Retrieve command to retrieve a file

(F7); or you can press the Zero key to indicate that you don't want to perform any of the numbered options.

How to use the Retrieve command to retrieve a file

Another way to retrieve a file is to use the Retrieve command. If you look at the command template, you'll find it right above the Save command. To access it, you use the Shift+F10 keystroke combination.

Like the Save command, this command works best when the default directory is set to the one that you want to use for your files. Then, the file specification that you give doesn't have to include the drive and directory. Instead, you just supply the file name.

Figure 2-4 shows you how to use this command to Retrieve a file when the default directory is set the way you want it. In step 1, you access the command. In step 2, you enter the name of the file that you want to retrieve and press the Enter key. Of course, this assumes that you know the name of the file. If you do, you can usually retrieve a file more quickly with this command for release 5.1 than you can with the List command. If you don't know the file name, you can use the List command to both find and retrieve the file.

Unlike the Retrieve function for the List command, the Retrieve command for release 5.1 doesn't display a warning message when you're about to retrieve a file into a document that isn't empty. It just retrieves the file into the current document at the cursor location.

How to move the cursor more efficiently

In the last unit, you learned how to use the Arrow keys to move the cursor through existing text. Often, though, you can move the cursor more efficiently by using the keystroke combinations shown in figure 2-5. As a result, it's worth taking the time to memorize these combinations.

Keystrokes	Function
The Control key and the Arrow keys	
Ctrl+Right	Moves the cursor right one word at a time
Ctrl+Left	Moves the cursor left one word at a time
Ctrl+Up (5.1)	Moves the cursor up one paragraph at a time
Ctrl+Down (5.1)	Moves the cursor down one paragraph at a time
The Home key and the Arrow keys	
Home Left	Moves the cursor to the left of the line after all codes
Home Right	Moves the cursor to the right of the line after all codes
Home Up	Moves the cursor to the top of the Edit screen
Home Down	Moves the cursor to the bottom of the Edit screen
Home Home Up	Moves the cursor to the top of the document after all codes
Home Home Home Up	Moves the cursor to the top of the document before all codes
Home Home Down	Moves the cursor to the bottom of the document after all codes
Home Home Home Left	Moves the cursor to the left of the line before all codes
The End key	
End	Moves the cursor to the right of the line after all codes

Figure 2-5   How to move the cursor efficiently

If you hold down the Ctrl key as you use the Right and Left arrow keys, the cursor jumps one word at a time. If you're using *WordPerfect* 5.1, you can also use the Up and Down arrow keys while you hold down the Ctrl key. These keys jump the cursor up and down one complete paragraph.

If you press the Home key one or more times followed by an Arrow key, you get the movement shown in the second group in figure 2-5. If, for example, you press the Home key once followed by the Left or Right arrow key, the cursor moves to the left or right of a line. If you press the Home key once followed by the Up or Down arrow keys, the cursor moves to the top or bottom of the Edit screen.

If you press the Home key twice followed by the Up arrow key, the cursor moves to the top of the document before any text, but after any control

Keystrokes	Function
Ctrl+Backspace	Deletes the word the cursor is on
Ctrl+Delete	Deletes the word the cursor is on
Ctrl+End	Deletes all text and codes from the cursor to the end of the line
Ctrl+Page-down	Deletes all text and codes from the cursor to the end of the page

Figure 2-6   How to use the control keys to delete text

codes. If you press the Home key three times, though, followed by the Up arrow key, the cursor moves to the top of the document before both codes and text. Similarly, pressing the Home key twice followed by the Down arrow moves the cursor to the end of the document after both text and codes. And pressing the Home key three times followed by the Left arrow moves the cursor to the left of a line before any codes. As you use more codes, you'll realize that there are times when you want to move the cursor before the codes at the top or left of a document, and there are times when you want to move it after the codes but before the text.

The last key in figure 2-5 is the End key. When you press this key, it moves the cursor to the right of a line after all codes. This is the same as pressing the Home key once followed by the Right arrow key, but you'll usually use the End key for this purpose because it takes only one keystroke.

How to delete more efficiently

In the last unit, you learned how to delete by using the Backspace key and the Delete key. However, you can usually delete text more quickly by using the keystroke combinations shown in figure 2-6. As a result, you should take the time to memorize these combinations so you can work more efficiently.

To delete an entire word at a time, you can press either the Backspace or Delete key while you hold down the Ctrl key. This deletes the word at the cursor. For this purpose, a *word* is any group of characters that is preceded and followed by one or more spaces. When you use this keystroke combination, the cursor doesn't have to be at the first character of the word; it can be anywhere in the word. If you use the Ctrl key with the Arrow keys to find the words that you want to delete, you just continue to hold down the Ctrl key while you press the Delete or Backspace key to delete one or more of the words.

If you press the End key while you hold down the Ctrl key, *WordPerfect* deletes all the characters from the location of the cursor to the end of the

1. Move the cursor to where you want to restore text that was deleted. Then, access the Cancel command (F1). This displays the last deletion at the cursor and this prompt:

   Undelete: 1 Restore; **2** Previous Deletion: **0**

2. To restore the deleted text that's shown at the cursor, press *1* or *r*.
3. To restore a previous deletion, press *2* or *p* to display it at the cursor. Remember, you can restore up to two previous deletions. When the text you want to restore is shown above the prompt, press *1* or *r* to restore it.

Figure 2-7   How to use the Cancel command to restore text

line. Similarly, if you press the Page-down key while you hold down the Ctrl key, *WordPerfect* deletes all the characters and codes from the location of the cursor to the end of the page. In this case, though, *WordPerfect* displays a prompt like this:

Delete Remainder of Page? No (Yes)

This warns you that the remainder of the page is about to be deleted. Then, if you don't want to delete the remainder of the page, press *n* for No. If you do, press *y* for Yes.

How to use the Cancel command to restore codes and text that have been deleted

As you develop your *WordPerfect* skills, you start to work more quickly and less cautiously. As a result, you occasionally delete a portion of a document by accident. Fortunately, though, *WordPerfect* provides a feature that lets you *restore* the text and codes that you have deleted in any one of your last three deletions. This puts the text and codes back into the document at the location of the cursor.

Figure 2-7 gives the procedure for restoring text. In step 1, you move the cursor to the point at which you want to restore a deletion. Then, you access the Cancel command (F1). *WordPerfect* then displays the last deletion that you made at the cursor location, and it displays the prompt shown in figure 2-7.

If the deletion shown is the one that you want to restore, just press *1* or *r* to restore it as shown in step 2. If it isn't, you press *2* or *p* to see the previous deletion. When you do this, *WordPerfect* displays the previous deletion at the cursor location and continues to display the prompt shown in figure 2-7. Then, if it still isn't the right deletion, you can press *2* or *p* to see the third

---

1. Position the cursor where you want to insert the date. Then, access the Date/Outline command (Shift+F5) to display this prompt:

    1 Date **T**ext; **2** Date **C**ode; **3** Date **F**ormat; **4 O**utline; **5** Para Num; **6 D**efine: **0**

2. As you can see, the first three options are for the Date command and the last three are for the Outline command. To insert the date, select Date Text by pressing *1* or *t*, or select Date Code by pressing *2* or *c*. If you want to change the date format, select Date Format (*3* or *f*) before you select Date Text or Date Code.

Figure 2-8   How to use the Date command to insert the current date into a document

most recent deletion. If you continue to press *2* or *p*, *WordPerfect* will cycle through the three most recent deletions again. When you press *1* or *r*, the deletion that is shown is restored. To cancel the command without restoring text, you can press the Esc, Cancel (F1), or Zero key.

How to use the Date command to insert the current date into a document

Most PCs today automatically keep track of the current date and time. On the older PCs, you are asked to enter the correct date and time as part of the DOS start-up procedure. But either way, the current date is available to *WordPerfect*, and you can insert it in your documents without typing it.

Figure 2-8 shows how to insert the current date into a document. In step 1, you move the cursor to where you want the date inserted. Then, you access both the Date and Outline commands by finding the Date/Outline key (Shift+F5) on the template and pressing it. This displays a prompt with three date options:

1 Date Text; 2 Date Code; 3 Date Format

The other options in the prompt are for the Outline command, not the Date command.

In step 2, if you select the Date Text option, the current date is inserted in your document just as if you typed it. This way, you don't have to manually enter the date. If you select the Date Code option, though, a date code is inserted in your document. This code is automatically updated each time you retrieve the document. This is useful when you work on a document over several days, and you always want the document printed with the current date.

The third date option in the prompt is Date Format. You can use this option to set the format of the date before you use options *1* or *2*. You can use the Date Format option to display the date in several formats including

1. Move the cursor to the sentence or paragraph that you want to move, copy, or delete. For a sentence, the cursor can be anywhere from the first letter of a the sentence to the period. For a paragraph, the cursor can be anywhere from the first letter of the paragraph to the hard return code [HRt] at the end of the paragraph.

2. Access the Move command (Ctrl+F4) to display this prompt:

   Move: 1 **S**entence; **2 P**aragraph; **3 P**age; **4 R**etrieve: **0**

3. Select Sentence or Paragraph by pressing the related highlighted number or letter. Then, the sentence or paragraph that the cursor is in is highlighted, and *WordPerfect* displays this prompt:

   1 Move; **2 C**opy; **3 D**elete; **4 A**ppend: **0**

4. Select Move, Copy, or Delete by pressing the related number or letter. If you select Move, the highlighted sentence or paragraph is removed from the screen, and this prompt is displayed:

   Move cursor; press **Enter** to retrieve.

   If you select Copy, the highlighting is removed from the sentence or paragraph, and the prompt shown above is displayed. If you select Delete, the highlighted sentence or paragraph is removed from the screen, and the command is finished.

5. If you selected Move or Copy, position the cursor where you want to insert the text and press the Enter key.

Figure 2-9   How to use the Move command to move, copy, or delete a sentence or paragraph

this one: mm/dd/yy. You can also include the time of day in the format. Usually, though, the format for the date is set the way you want it so you probably won't have to use this third option.

How to use the Move command to move, copy, or delete a sentence or a paragraph

You can use the Move command to move a sentence or a paragraph from one part of a document to another. However, you can also use this command to Copy or Delete a sentence or a paragraph. In fact, the most efficient way to move, copy, or delete a sentence or paragraph is to use the Move command.

Figure 2-9 shows you how to use the Move command for any of these three functions. In step 1, you move the cursor to the sentence or paragraph that you want to move, copy, or delete. To operate on a sentence, the cursor can be anywhere from the first character in the sentence to the period. To operate on a paragraph, the cursor can be anywhere from the first character of the paragraph to the hard return code at the end of the paragraph.

In step 2, you access the Move command (Ctrl+F4). This displays the prompt shown in figure 2-9. Then, in step 3, you select either Sentence or Paragraph. When you do this, the entire sentence or paragraph at the cursor is highlighted, and the second prompt in figure 2-9 is displayed.

In step 4, you select either Move, Copy, or Delete. If you select Move, the highlighted sentence or paragraph disappears from the Edit screen and is copied into *WordPerfect*'s memory. If you select Copy, the highlighting disappears, but the text remains. If you select Delete, the highlighted sentence or paragraph disappears and you are returned to the Edit screen.

In step 5, you continue with the function if you selected Move or Copy in step 4. Then, you move the cursor to the point where you want the sentence or paragraph moved or copied to. To complete the function, you press the Enter key.

It may take a bit of practice using the Move or Copy functions before you are able to move the cursor to exactly the right spot before pressing the Enter key. When you move a sentence, for example, you should note that the sentence includes the spaces after it. As a result, you need to move the cursor to the first character of the sentence you want to insert the new sentence in front of before you press the Enter key. If you don't get the Move or Copy function quite right, though, you can make whatever corrections are needed.

How to use the Block command

The Block command is used to identify a block of text that you want to perform a function on. After you identify the *block*, you can perform various *WordPerfect* functions on it. For instance, you can delete, move, or copy it. In addition, you can insert paired codes around the block.

How to use the Block command to block text   The first procedure in figure 2-10 shows you how to block text. In step 1, you move the cursor to the start of the text that you want to block. In step 2, you access the Block command by pressing F12 if you have the 101-key keyboard or Alt+F4 if you don't. This displays a flashing prompt that says "Block On." In step 3, you move the cursor to the end of the text that you want to block. At this point, you haven't performed a function yet, but the block has been identified and the prompt is still flashing.

To move the cursor as efficiently as possible when you're blocking text, you just press the character that you want the cursor to jump to. If, for example, you press the Period key, the cursor jumps to the next period in the text. As a result, this is an efficient way to block to the end of the sentence. Similarly, if you press the Enter key, the cursor jumps to the next hard return code [HRt] in the text. As a result, this is an efficient way to block to the end of the paragraph. With a little practice, you can highlight blocks more quickly this way than you can using the normal keystroke combinations for cursor movement.

How to perform functions on a block   The second, third, and fourth procedures in figure 2-10 show you how to perform functions on a block. To delete a block, for example, you just press the Delete key as summarized in the second procedure. Then, when the prompt asks for confirmation, you press *y* for Yes. This deletes the block and returns you to the Edit screen.

To move or copy a block, you use the Move command as summarized in the third procedure in figure 2-10. After you access the Move command, you press *1* or *b* to indicate that you want to operate on the block. Then, you select either the Move or Copy function. To complete the command, you position the cursor where you want the block inserted and press the Enter key.

To insert paired codes around a block, just access the related command. If, for example, you want to boldface a block, press F6 for the Bold command. If you want to underline a block, press F8 for the Underline command.

These examples are designed to show you how you can perform functions on blocks of text. But they aren't the only functions you can perform. For instance, you can use the Print command to print a block and the Save command to save a block. To use one of these commands after you've blocked the text, just access the command and do whatever the prompts require. If you try to perform a command that isn't appropriate for a block, your attempt to access the command will be ignored.

Because the Move command is designed for moving, copying, or deleting sentences, paragraphs, and pages, you don't need the Block command for these operations. Instead, you should use the Block command when you want to move, copy, or delete odd portions of text like part of one paragraph plus the two full paragraphs that follow it.

How to use the Format command

When you create a new document with *WordPerfect*, it automatically formats the document according to its *default settings*, or just *defaults*. If, however, the default settings aren't appropriate for your purposes, you can use the Format command to override them for any document you work on. If you look at the command template, you can see that you access the Format command by using the Shift+F8 keystroke combination. This displays the Format screen shown in figure 2-11. Although this screen has many words on it, there are only four options: Line, Page, Document, and Other. To access one of them, you type the number or letter of the option. In this unit, though, I'm going to show you how to use only the Line and Page formats.

How to use the Block command to block text

1. Position the cursor where you want to begin the block.
2. Access the Block command (F12 or Alt+F4); then, this flashing prompt is displayed:
   `Block On`
3. Move the cursor to the last character of the block. The characters within the block are highlighted as you move the cursor.

How to use the Delete key to delete a block

1. Block the text you want to delete.
2. Press the Delete key; then, this prompt is displayed:
   `Delete block? No (Yes)`
3. Press *y* for yes and the blocked text is deleted.

How to use the Move command to move or copy a block

1. Block the text you want to move or copy.
2. Access the Move command (Ctrl+F4) to display this prompt:
   `Move: 1 Block; 2 Tabular Column; 3 Rectangle:   0`
3. Select Block by pressing *1* or *b*; then, this prompt is displayed:
   `1 Move; 2 Copy; 3 Delete; 4 Append: 0`
4. Select Move or Copy by pressing the related number or letter; then, this prompt is displayed:
   `Move cursor; press Enter to retrieve.`
5. Position the cursor where you want to insert the text and press the Enter key.

How to insert paired codes on each side of a block

1. Block the text you want to code.
2. Access the paired code you want to insert. For example, press F8 for underline or F6 for boldface. This inserts the paired codes on each side of the block. As a result, the blocked text is boldfaced or underlined when the document is printed.

Figure 2-10   How to use the Block command

When you access the Line or Page option, you get the Line or Page screen shown in figure 2-12. The settings shown on these screens are the default settings for your system. As you can see in this figure, the Line screen has nine options; the Page screen has eight. If you're using *WordPerfect* 5.0,

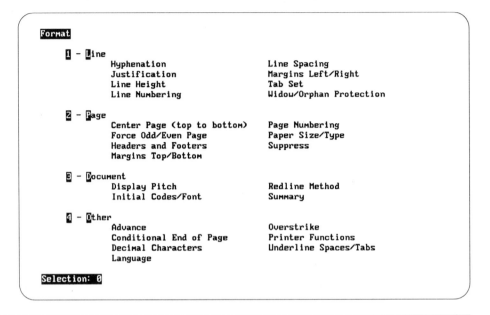

```
┌─────────────────────────────────────────────────────────────────────┐
│ Format                                                                │
│                                                                       │
│    1 - Line                                                           │
│                Hyphenation                    Line Spacing            │
│                Justification                  Margins Left/Right      │
│                Line Height                    Tab Set                 │
│                Line Numbering                 Widow/Orphan Protection │
│                                                                       │
│    2 - Page                                                           │
│                Center Page (top to bottom)    Page Numbering          │
│                Force Odd/Even Page            Paper Size/Type         │
│                Headers and Footers            Suppress                │
│                Margins Top/Bottom                                     │
│                                                                       │
│    3 - Document                                                       │
│                Display Pitch                  Redline Method          │
│                Initial Codes/Font             Summary                 │
│                                                                       │
│    4 - Other                                                          │
│                Advance                        Overstrike              │
│                Conditional End of Page        Printer Functions       │
│                Decimal Characters             Underline Spaces/Tabs   │
│                Language                                                │
│                                                                       │
│ Selection: 0                                                          │
└─────────────────────────────────────────────────────────────────────┘
```

Figure 2-11   The main Format screen

your Page screen has nine options, but this doesn't affect the skills presented in this unit, so you can ignore the difference for now.

When you change one of the Line or Page options, *WordPerfect* inserts a code that controls the formatting of the document. As a result, you should be sure to put the cursor where you want the code to be inserted before you access the Format command. Since some of these codes only affect text below them and others only work right if they're at the start of a document, you insert most formatting codes at the start of a document.

If the codes you insert don't work the way you want them to, you can use the Reveal Codes command that you learned about in the last unit. Then, you can insert, delete, and correct the placement of the codes so they work correctly.

How to set Line options   Figure 2-13 summarizes the procedures for changing three of the Line options. These are the options that you're most likely to change.

The first procedure in figure 2-13 shows you how to change the *justification* for a document. This term refers to the alignment of the text when it's printed, although this alignment doesn't appear on the Edit screen. In figure 2-1, for example, the letter is printed with *justified text*. This means

The Line screen

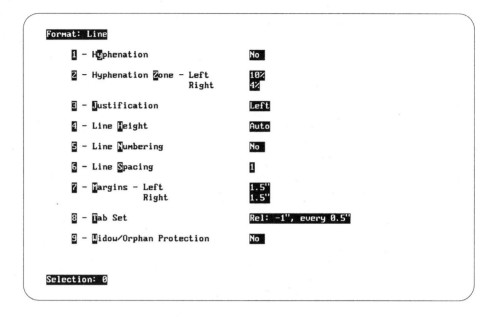

The Page screen

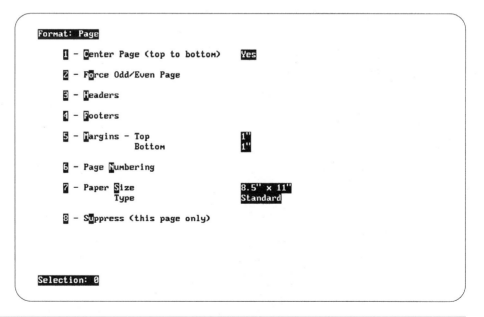

Figure 2-12   The Line and Page screens of the Format command

that the text is flush with both the left and right margins. You can see this most clearly in the first and last paragraphs of the letter. In contrast, the same letter is printed without justification in figure 2-17. This type of printing can be referred to as *ragged-right text*.

For simple business documents like letters, ragged-right text is preferable to justified text for a couple of reasons. First, studies have shown that ragged-right text is easier to read than justified text. Second, studies have shown that letters are more effective when they don't have the formal appearance that is associated with justified text. So if your default setting is for justified text, that's the first Line option that you should change.

To change this option, just follow the first procedure in figure 2-13. When you reach the Line format screen, select the Justification option by pressing *3* or *j*. Unfortunately, though, the *WordPerfect* 5.1 terminology for justification differs from the traditional typesetting terminology. So to set the justification for ragged right when using release 5.1, select the Left option from the four given in the prompt. This means that the text should be aligned on the left margin only. For *WordPerfect* 5.0, type *n* for No. This means that the justification should be turned off.

If you use the Reveal Codes screen when you return to the Edit screen, you can see the justification codes that *WordPerfect* has inserted. Depending on which release of *WordPerfect* you're using, your code will look like one of these:

[Just Off] or [Just:Left].

The second procedure in figure 2-13 shows you how to set the left and the right margins for a document. You'll probably change the Margins option more often than any of the other Line options because the margins help determine how much can be printed on a page. To get more on a page, you just decrease the size of the margins.

When you reach the Line screen, you select the Margins option by pressing *7* or *m*. The cursor then moves to the entry for the Left margin. If you want to leave it the way it is, press the Enter key to move to the entry for the Right margin. Otherwise, type the value that you want for the Left margin and press Enter. Next, type the value for the Right margin, or leave it as is if it's the way you want it. Then, when you press the Enter key, the margin code is inserted into the document, and the cursor moves to the selection prompt at the bottom of the Line screen.

If the measurements on your system are set for inches, you enter decimal numbers for the left and right margins. For instance, 1.25 means 1-1/4 inches, and 1.75 means 1-3/4 inches. If the measurements are set for units, you enter numbers that represent the number of characters that should be skipped on the left and right margins. For instance, 15 means that 15 characters should be skipped. Then, if your system is set for printing at 10

How to set the justification to ragged-right

1. Move the cursor to the top of the document by pressing Home Home Up.
2. Access the Format command (Shift+F8). This displays the screen shown in figure 2-11.
3. Select the Line option. This displays the Line screen shown in figure 2-12.
4. Select the Justification option. If you're using release 5.1, select the Left option from the prompt that's displayed:

   Justification: 1 Left; 2 Center; 3 Right; 4 Full: 0

   If you're using release 5.0, just type *n* for No.
5. Press the Exit key (F7) to return to the Edit screen.

How to set the left and right margins

1. Move the cursor to the top of the document by pressing Home Home Up.
2. Access the Format command (Shift+F8). This displays the screen shown in figure 2-11.
3. Select the Line option. This displays the Line screen shown in figure 2-12.
4. Select the Margins option.
5. If your system is set for inches, type the decimal number for the number of inches you want for the Left margin and press the Enter key. Then, repeat this procedure for the Right margin. If you type 1.25, for example, the margin will be 1-1/4 inches.

   If your system is set for units, type the number of units you want for the Left margin and press the Enter key. Then, repeat the procedure for the Right margin. If you type the number 15, for example, the margin is set to 15 characters. Then, if your system is set to print at 10 characters per inch, this sets the margin at 1-1/2 inches. If your system is set to print at 12 characters per inch, this sets the margin at 1-1/4 inches.
6. Press the Exit key (F7) to return to the Edit screen.

How to set the line spacing for double spacing

1. Move the cursor to the top of the document by pressing Home Home Up.
2. Access the Format command (Shift+F8).
3. Select the Line option from the Format screen.
4. Select the Line Spacing option from the Line screen.
5. Type *2* for double spacing and press the Enter key.
6. Press the Exit key (F7) to return to the Edit screen.

Figure 2-13   How to set three Line options of the Format command

characters per inch, 15 units leads to a 1-1/2 inch margin; if your system is set for printing at 12 characters per inch, 15 units leads to a 1-1/4 inch margin.

In general, you should set the margins to print fewer than 66 characters in each line. This makes your document easier to read. If your system is set for printing at 10 characters per inch, margins of about 1 inch (10 units) are appropriate. If your system is set for printing at 12 characters per inch, margins of about 1.5 inches (18 units) are appropriate. If you're using a printer that doesn't print a set number of characters per inch, you may have to count the characters in a line or two to see how many characters a typical line contains. Then, you can adjust your margins accordingly.

Although inches and units are the most commonly used measurements, *WordPerfect* also provides for measurements in centimeters, picas, or points. The last two of these measurements are used only in desktop publishing applications, though, so I doubt that the default setting on your system is for one of them.

If you reveal codes when you return to the Edit screen, you can see that *WordPerfect* inserts a code like one of these into the document:

[L/R Mar:1.5i,1.5i] or [L/R Mar:18,18]

Here, the first code is in inches, and the second one is in units.

The third procedure in figure 2-13 shows you how to change the line spacing for a document from single to double spacing. This is useful if you're preparing a report (like a college paper) that has to be double spaced or if you want to have extra room for editorial marks on a preliminary draft of a document. In steps 1 through 4, you move the cursor to the top of the document; you access the Format command; you select the Line option; and you select the Line Spacing option. In step 5, you type *2* for double spacing and press the Enter key. In step 6, you exit from the command.

When you specify double spacing, the lines on the screen are double spaced. As a result, the Edit screen can only display half as much text when this option is on as it can otherwise. For this reason, you probably won't want to set the code for double spacing until you're ready to print the document. While you work on the document, you'll want to keep the code set for single spacing.

How to set Page options   Figure 2-14 summarizes the procedures for changing two of the Page options. These are the two options that you're most likely to change. The first procedure in figure 2-14 shows you how to center a page from top to bottom. When you reach the Page screen, you select the Center Page option by pressing *1* or *c*. Then, if you're using *WordPerfect* 5.0, the option is turned on right away. But if you're using *WordPerfect* 5.1, you have to press *y* for Yes before the option is turned on. In either case, the cursor returns to the selection prompt at the bottom of the Page screen.

How to center the printed page from top to bottom

1. Move the cursor to the top of the document by pressing Home Home Up.
2. Access the Format command (Shift+F8). This displays the screen shown in figure 2-11.
3. Select the Page option. This displays the Format Page screen shown in figure 2-12.
4. Select the Center Page option. If you're using release 5.1, press *y* for Yes at this prompt to turn on the option:

    No (Yes)

    If you're using release 5.0, the option is turned on automatically when you select the Center Page option .
5. Press the Exit key (F7) to return to the Edit screen.

How to set the top and bottom margins for the printed page

1. Move the cursor to the top of the document by pressing Home Home Up.
2. Access the Format command (Shift+F8). This displays the Format screen shown in figure 2-11.
3. Select the Page option. This displays the Format Page screen shown in figure 2-12.
4. Select the Margins option.
5. If your system is set for inches, type the decimal number for the number of inches you want for the Top margin and press the Enter key. Then, repeat this procedure for the Bottom margin. If you type 1, for example, the margin will be 1 inch. If you type 1.5, the margin will be 1-1/2 inches.

    If your system is set for units, type the number of units you want for the Top margin and press the Enter key. Then, repeat this procedure for the Bottom margin. If you type the number 6, for example, the margin will be set at 6 lines. Since a standard printer prints 6 lines per inch, this sets the Top and Bottom margins at 1 inch.
6. Press the Exit key (F7) to return to the Edit screen.

Figure 2-14   How to set two Page options of the Format command

If you reveal codes, you will see that the code for page centering looks like this: [Center Pg]. Later, when the document is printed, it will be centered on the page with equal amounts of space above and below the printed text. This option is especially useful for letters because it helps make them look more appealing.

The second procedure in figure 2-14 shows how to set the Top and Bottom margins for each page of a document. If you reveal codes after you

Keystroke	Function
Highlighted letter or number	Selects an option
Esc	Returns to the previous screen
Cancel (F1)	Returns to the previous screen
Zero (0)	Returns to the previous screen
Exit (F7)	Returns to the Edit screen

Figure 2-15   Keystrokes you can use to move between command screens

set the margins, you will see a code like one of these for the Top and Bottom margins: [T/B:1i,1i] or [T/B:6,6].

In terms of inches, a one-inch margin is appropriate for most business documents. In terms of units, which represent lines when they're applied to Top and Bottom margins, 6 is the equivalent of a one-inch margin because most printers print six lines to the inch.

How to move from one screen to another within a command

With the Format command, you've seen how one screen can lead to another after you access a command. To move between these command screens efficiently, you should use the keystrokes that are summarized in figure 2-15.

To move from one screen to the next, you select an option by pressing the highlighted letter or number for the option. Then, to go back one screen, you can press the Esc key or the Cancel key (F1). On most screens, you can also press the Zero key (0) to indicate that you're not making any selection. And if you want to return immediately to the Edit screen without going back through the screens one at a time, you can press the Exit key (F7).

If you press the Esc key when you're not trying to escape from a command or a screen, you may be surprised to see a message on the left side of the status line. Although the number may be different, the message looks like this:

Repeat Value = 8

This means you've accessed a function that is designed to repeat whatever you enter next. If, for example, you press the letter *w* while the message is displayed, eight *w*'s will be entered into your document. You can cancel the repeat function by pressing the Esc key again.

Discussion   You have now been introduced to seven new commands as well as several keystroke combinations that will help you move the cursor and delete text more efficiently. If you combine these commands and skills with those in unit 1, you should be able to retrieve and modify the letter that you created in the last unit. You should be able to add a sentence and a paragraph to it so it looks like the letter in figure 2-16. You should be able to use the Move command to edit the letter in figure 2-16 so it looks like the one in figure 2-17. And when you've got the letter the way you want it, you should be able to print it and save it under its old name.

If you feel confident about your *WordPerfect* skills already, you should be able to make the changes shown in figures 2-16 and 2-17 without any help. But if you don't feel confident, do the exercises at the end of this unit. The first ten exercises guide you through some experimentation with commands and keystrokes that you probably won't do on your own. Then, the last three exercises guide you through the steps of the revision process.

Once you master all of the skills presented in units 1 and 2, you will have a respectable set of *WordPerfect* skills. You have already learned how to use 15 of the most useful *WordPerfect* commands. And since there are only 40 keystroke combinations on the template, this means that you're well on the way to *WordPerfect* proficiency. In the next unit, you'll learn how to use seven more commands and a few more keystroke combinations. After that, you'll be on your way to *WordPerfect* mastery.

Terms

default directory	default
restore	justification
block	justified text
default setting	ragged-right text

Objectives

1. Use the new commands presented in this unit to perform any of the following functions:

   a) Change the default directory.
   b) Retrieve a file.
   c) Restore text that has recently been deleted.
   d) Insert the current date into a document in either text or code form.
   e) Move, copy, or delete a sentence or paragraph.
   f) Move, copy, or delete a block of text.
   g) Insert paired codes on the sides of a block of text.
   h) Set the line or page margins for a printed document.
   i) Vertically center a document on a printed page.
   j) Set the justification code so the document is printed with ragged right text.

August 20, 1992

Dear :

    Thanks for asking about our PC books. I've enclosed a catalog that describes them all in detail. As you read through it, I hope you'll find something you can use right away.

    So there's no risk to you, all our books are backed by our unconditional guarantee:

    You must be satisfied. If our PC books aren't the best ones you've ever used for both training and reference, you can return them for a full refund. <u>No questions asked</u>.

    Our best-selling PC title, <u>The Least You Need to Know about DOS</u>, is described on page 7. Our newest book, <u>The Least You Need to Know about Lotus</u>, is described on page 8. The descriptions in the catalog will help you decide if one of these books is right for you or your company.

    If you have any questions or if you're ready to place an order, please call us at our toll-free number: 1-800-221-5528. And thanks for your interest in our books.

    Sincerely,

    Karen DeMartin

Figure 2-16   The letter in figure 2-1 after it has been retrieved, edited, and printed

August 20, 1992

Dear :

        Thanks for asking about our PC books. I've
enclosed a catalog that describes them all in detail.
As you read through it, I hope you'll find something
you can use right away.

        Our newest book, <u>The Least You Need to Know about
Lotus</u>, is described on page 8. Our best-selling PC
title, <u>The Least You Need to Know about DOS</u>, is
described on page 7. The descriptions in the catalog
will help you decide if one of these books is right for
you or your company.

        So there's no risk to you, all our books are
backed by our unconditional guarantee:

        <u>You must be satisfied</u>. If our PC books
        aren't the best ones you've ever used for
        both training and reference, you can return
        them for a full refund. <u>No questions asked</u>.

        If you have any questions or if you're ready to
place an order, please call us at our toll-free number:
1-800-221-5528. And thanks for your interest in our
books.

                Sincerely,

                Karen DeMartin

Figure 2-17   The letter in figure 2-16 after it has been edited and printed

2. Use any of the skills or commands presented in this unit or the previous unit to modify a document in ways that are similar to those indicated by figures 2-16 and 2-17.

Exercises

Part 1: How to use the new commands and keystrokes

1. Start *WordPerfect* and access the List command by pressing F5. *WordPerfect* then displays a prompt at the bottom of the screen in this form:

    Dir C:\WP50*.*

    The directory shown is the *default directory*. If this is the directory that you want to store your document files in, press the Cancel key (F1) to cancel the command and return to the Edit screen. But if it isn't, press equals (=) to change the directory. *WordPerfect* then displays a prompt in this form:

    New Directory = C:\WP50

    To change the directory, just type the drive and path for the directory that you want; it will replace the directory shown. Or if you prefer, modify the directory shown by using the Arrow keys, typeover or insert mode, and so on. When the drive and directory are correct, press the Enter key to complete the change of directory. Then, press the Esc or Cancel key (F1) to return to the Edit screen.

2. Access the List command again. This time, when *WordPerfect* displays the default directory at the bottom of the screen, it should be the one you want for your files. Then, press the Enter key to tell *WordPerfect* that you want it to display the List screen for that directory. If you saved your files correctly at the end of the last unit, your List screen should display the two files in figure 2-3.

3. Use the Arrow keys to move the highlight from one file to another. When the highlight is on the file named CATLET (not CATLET.FM), press the Enter key. This starts the Look function, which lets you review the contents of the file. Press Enter again to return to the List screen. Then, press *1* or *r* to retrieve the file. This returns you to the Edit screen with the CATLET document displayed on the screen.

4. Use the keystroke combinations shown in figure 2-5 to move the cursor through the letter. To start, use the Ctrl+Right arrow key combination to move the cursor forward one word at a time. Then, use the Ctrl+Left arrow key combination to move the cursor backwards one word at a time. If you're using *WordPerfect* 5.1, continue to hold the Ctrl key down as you experiment with the Up and Down arrow keys. Do they jump the cursor up and down one paragraph at a time?
    Now, use the Home key combinations shown in figure 2-5 to move the cursor to the left of a line, to the right of a line, to the top of the

screen, to the bottom of the screen, and to the end of the document. Next, try two Homes and an Up to move the cursor to the top of the document. Last, move the cursor to the start of the second paragraph in the body of the letter. Then, press the End key to move the cursor to the end of the line.

5. Use the keystroke combinations in figure 2-6 to delete text. To start, hold the Ctrl key down and press the Right arrow key to move to the word *or* in the first sentence of the last paragraph of the letter. When you reach it, continue to hold down the Ctrl key. Then, press the Backspace key to delete the word; press the Backspace key three more times to delete the next three words; and press the Delete key four more times to delete the words through *an order*. Note that the comma is deleted along with the word *order*, so release the Ctrl key and re-enter the comma in the appropriate place.

Move the cursor to the start of the second paragraph in the letter. Next, hold down the Ctrl key and press the End key. This deletes the entire line. Press the Delete key by itself to move the cursor to the next line, and use the Ctrl+End key combination again to delete that line.

Now, hold down the Ctrl key and press the Page-down key. When the prompt asks whether you want to delete the remainder of the page, press *y* for Yes. Is the rest of the document gone?

To restore it, press the Cancel key. This shows the last deletion starting at the cursor location. But press the letter *p* to show the previous deletion, and press it two more times to return to the first deletion. Then, press the letter *r* to restore the highlighted text.

6. With the restored document on the Edit screen, access the List command. Then, move the highlight to CATLET and press *r* for the Retrieve function. Since a document is already on the screen, *WordPerfect* displays this prompt:

Retrieve into current document? No (Yes)

Type *n* for No, and you are returned to the Edit screen.

Next, use the Retrieve command to retrieve CATLET. If you're using release 5.0, you get the warning prompt that's shown above. For this exercise, press *y* for Yes to retrieve the document. If you're using release 5.1, however, you don't get the warning prompt and the document is instantly retrieved into the current document. When you return to the Edit screen, you'll see that you have a mess.

No problem, though. Clear the screen by accessing the Exit command (F7), pressing *n* to indicate that you don't want to save the file, and pressing *n* again to indicate that you don't want to exit from the program. This returns you to a blank Edit screen. Then, use the Retrieve command again to retrieve CATLET. Since the changes (deletions) that you made in exercise 5 were never saved, the document is just as you left it at the end of the last unit.

7. Move the cursor to the first character in the date of CATLET. Press Reveal Codes to look at the characters in the date, and press Reveal Codes again to return to the normal Edit screen. With the cursor still at the first character in the date, use Ctrl+End to delete the date. Then, start the Date command (Shift+F5), and press 2 or c to insert the date code into the document. Press Reveal codes to look at the date code, and press the Backspace key one time to delete the code and the entire date with it. Last, start the Date command again, and press *1* or *t* to insert the date text into the document. This time, characters are inserted just as if you had typed the date. Press Reveal Codes to return to the normal Edit screen.

8. Move the cursor to the middle of the first sentence in the first paragraph in the letter. Use the Move command to delete the sentence. To do that, start the command (Ctrl+F4); press the highlighted number or letter for Sentence; and press the highlighted number or letter for Delete. The sentence is gone.

   Next, use the Move command to copy the paragraph that the cursor is in. Start the command; press *2* for Paragraph; press *2* for Copy; press Home Home Down to move the cursor to the end of the document; and press Enter to complete the copy function.

   To clear the screen, use the Exit command. Then, use the Retrieve command to retrieve CATLET one more time in its original form.

9. Move the cursor to the start of the underlined phrase, "No questions asked." Then, press Reveal Codes, move the cursor to the Underline code at the start of the phrase, press the Delete key to delete the underlining, and press Reveal Codes again to return to the normal Edit screen.

   Next, move the cursor to the first letter of the phrase. Then, start the Block command (Alt+F4 or F12). To jump the cursor to the end of the sentence, press the Period key. To jump the cursor to the ends of the next paragraphs, press the Enter key a few times. This shows that *WordPerfect* will move the cursor to the first occurrence of whatever character you press. This helps you move the cursor more quickly. Now, press the Cancel key to cancel the blocking operation.

   Next, start the Block command again and highlight the entire phrase except the period. Then, press the Underline key (F8) to put the paired Underline codes around the phrase. This returns the letter to the way it was when you retrieved it.

10. Start the Format command (Shift+F8) to display the main Format screen. Then, press *p* to display the Page screen. The values shown are the default formatting options for your system. Are inches or units used for the top and bottom margins? What are the settings for these margins?

Press the Esc, Cancel, or Zero key to return to the main Format screen. Then, press *l* to display the Line screen. Here again, the values shown are the default formatting options for your system. Are inches or units used for the left and right margins? What are the settings for the Justification option and the left and right margins?

Press *m* to change the Margin settings. Enter new values that increase both the Left and Right margins by an inch or more. Then, press Exit to return to the Edit screen. Move the cursor up and down the screen to see how the margins change at the point where the margin code has been inserted into the document. Press Reveal Codes to see what the margin code looks like.

Move the cursor to the top of the document; start the Format command; and press *l* for Line options. Then, select the Line Spacing option; type *2*; press Enter; and press Exit to return to the Edit screen. Note how the lines on the screen are double spaced as you move the cursor through the document. Last, press the Reveal Codes and Exit keys. Then, press *n* twice to clear the Edit screen.

Part 2: How to retrieve and edit a letter

11. Use the List command to retrieve the file named CATLET.FM that you saved for the last unit. If necessary, change the default directory to the one for your files before you display the List screen and retrieve the document. To modify the document so it looks like the letter in figure 2-16, do the following.

    At the top of the letter, use the Date command to insert the date code, not the date text. That way, the form letter will always have the current date.

    Move the cursor to the start of the last paragraph in the body of the original letter. Then, use insert mode to insert the new paragraph that starts, "Our best-selling PC title..." into the letter. Next, move the cursor to the start of the indented guarantee, and type the new sentence shown in figure 2-16: "You must be satisfied." Last, use the Print command to print the revised letter.

12. Now, suppose that you decide to modify the revised the letter so it looks like the one in figure 2-17. To do that, use the Move command to move the new paragraph to the location shown in the figure. Then, use the Move command to switch the sequence of the second and third sentences in the new paragraph. Last, use the Block command to underline the new sentence in the guarantee.

13. Move the cursor to the top of the document. Then, start the Format command and move to the Line screen. If the Justification option isn't set

to Left (release 5.1) or Off (release 5.0), change it. Then, change the left and right margins so they're a half-inch larger. Press the Exit key twice to return to the Edit screen, and press Reveal Codes so you can see the codes that have been inserted at the top of the document.

Next, start the Format command again and move to the Page screen. Select the Center Page option and turn it on. Then, press the Zero key twice to return to the Edit screen. Note the code that has been inserted at the top of the document.

Last, print the letter again. Then, compare it to the letter you printed in exercise 11. Note the differences in the margins. And if you changed the Justification option too, note the differences in the way the paragraphs in the body of the letter are printed. To complete the exercises, save the revised document under its original name (CATLET.FM).

Unit 3

How to create and edit a two-page report

In units 1 and 2, you learned how to create and edit a one-page letter. Now, you'll learn how to work with multi-page documents. Along the way, you'll learn how to use seven more commands and some new keystroke combinations.

As you read this unit, you can try the *WordPerfect* skills it teaches on your own PC right after you read about them. Or you can read the entire unit first and then go through the exercises at the end of the unit. When you do the exercises, you will create a two-page report like the one in figure 3-1.

Five keystroke combinations for working with a multi-page document

Figure 3-2 presents some keystroke combinations that are useful when you're working on documents that are two or more pages long. You can press the Page-up or Page-down key to move the cursor to the top of the previous page or to the next page. If you press the Page-down key when you're on the last page of the document, the cursor moves to the end of the document after all codes.

When you hold down the Ctrl key and press the Home key, you access the Go-to function, which displays this prompt:

Go to

Then, when you type the number of the page that you want and press the Enter key, the cursor moves to that page.

The fourth keystroke combination in figure 3-2 is for the *hard page break*. When you type this key combination (Ctrl+Enter), *WordPerfect* inserts a hard page break code [HPg] into the document and a new page is started whether or not the previous page has been filled. In contrast, *WordPerfect* automatically inserts a *soft page break* [SPg] when it reaches the bottom of a page. As you can see in figure 3-3, a single dashed line on the Edit screen represents a soft page break, and a double dashed line represents a hard page break.

August 19, 1992   51REPORT   Page 1

Why we should upgrade from <u>WordPerfect</u> 5.0 to 5.1

Unlike <u>WordPerfect</u> 4.2 and 5.0, <u>WordPerfect</u> 5.0 and 5.1 share the same structure. Although some of the existing features have been enhanced, none of them have been drastically changed. <u>WordPerfect</u> 5.1 does, however, offer some new features including a Tables feature, Mouse support, and Pull-down menus.

At the end of this report, I'm going to recommend that our editors upgrade from <u>WordPerfect</u> 5.0 to 5.1. But first, I'm going to briefly describe the tables feature. I think that this feature alone makes it worthwhile to upgrade. I'm also going to present a brief analysis of the benefits and costs of converting to <u>WordPerfect</u> 5.1. When you finish this report, you can decide whether you would like more information on any of these subjects. If so, I'll be happy to get it for you.

The Tables feature The Tables feature can be used for several purposes, even as a simple spreadsheet. If you combine the Tables feature with the Math feature, for example, you can use formulas to calculate each cell within the table. However, the Tables feature is no substitute for a spreadsheet. It doesn't provide as many features as a spreadsheet, it's not as efficient, and it's not as easy to use.

However, the Tables feature is an efficient way to present tabular data. For example, we often use tables to present information in our reports. Right now, we use the Columns feature or Tabs to present this information, and we waste a lot of time. We set and reset our Tab stops until the table looks right. Or, we adjust and readjust the widths of the Columns feature. This can be tricky and time consuming. Since the Tables feature provides an easier way to adjust the width of each column in a table, it could save us a lot of time. The other day, for example, I used the Tables feature to create a table that I would have created with Tabs if I had been using 5.0. Although I'm still learning how to use the Tables feature, I finished this table in about five minutes.

Since a table like this used to take me about 20 minutes to create, I saved about 15 minutes on this table alone. If I'm right, converting to release 5.1 should save our editors about five to 20 minutes per table, depending on whether they are creating or editing the table. Since we need to create and edit many tables, I think converting to release 5.1 will save our editors time that is measurable in hours, not minutes.

The cost of converting to 5.1 The cost of upgrading to 5.1 will be about $85 per editor. In addition, the cost of converting from 5.0 to 5.1 includes the time it will take our editors to learn how to use the Tables feature. However, I think our editors can quickly learn how to use the Tables feature. In my opinion, the

Figure 3-1   A two-page report (part 1 of 2)

```
August 19, 1992          51REPORT                    Page 2
hard part of learning the Tables feature is learning how to use
the math functions to calculate data for each cell.  Since our
editors don't need to calculate any data, it shouldn't take an
editor more than an hour to learn how to use Tables.  The other
day, for example, I showed Monica how to use Tables.  After about
45 minutes of learning how to use the feature, she created her
first table in five minutes.

Analysis  If you calculate each editor's time to be worth $15 per
hour, I think you'll see that all of our editors should upgrade to
5.1 as soon as possible.  If you estimate that it will take each
editor an hour to learn how to use the Tables feature, the costs
of converting to 5.1, including training time, will be $100 per
editor.  If you assume that the Tables feature will save each
editor two hours a month, the savings for each editor will be $30
a month.  Therefore, the upgrade to 5.1 should pay for itself
within four or five months.  And since I'm confident these
estimates are conservative, the actual payback time should be even
shorter.
```

Figure 3-1   A two-page report (part 2 of 2)

You can use the fifth keystroke combination in figure 3-2 to insert an automatic page number into a document. To enter this code, you hold down the Ctrl key while you press the letter *b* (Ctrl+B). Then, the entry in the document looks like this:

^B

When you print your document, the correct page number is substituted for this code. As a result, this code prints as 1 on page 1, 2 on page 2, and so on.

How to set the Document options of the Format command

When you start a new document, it is given the default settings for your system. If, for example, the default settings for the left and right margins are one inch, a new document is given those settings. Then, if you want to change those defaults, you can use the Document options of the Format command. In contrast to the Line and Page options of the Format command, the Document options let you change the defaults for the entire document without inserting codes into the document.

Keystrokes	Function
Page-up	Moves the cursor to the top of the previous page
Page-down	Moves the cursor to the top of the next page
Ctrl+Home	Goes to the page number indicated by the entry that follows
Ctrl+Enter	Inserts a hard page break [HPg] into the document
Ctrl+B	Inserts an automatic page number (^B) into the document

Figure 3-2   Keystroke combinations for multi-page documents

Figure 3-4 displays the Document screen of the Format command. You reach this screen by accessing the Format command (Shift+F8) and selecting the Document option. Then, you can use the Initial Base Font option to select the font that you want to use for your document. And you can use the Initial Codes option to change the default settings for the entire document without inserting codes into the document. I'll show you how to use both of these options now.

How to set the Initial Base Font for a document   The third option on the Document screen is Initial Font for *WordPerfect* 5.0 and Initial Base Font for *WordPerfect* 5.1, but I'll refer to both as the Initial Base Font option from now on. In *WordPerfect* terms, the *font* is the type that is going to be used when the document is printed; the *base font* is the font that's in force as you work on a portion of a document; and the *initial base font* is the base font that is in force when you start work on a document.

To change the initial base font for a document when you're using a typical dot-matrix printer, you use the procedure that's summarized in figure 3-5. In step 1, you access the Initial Base Font option of the Format command. This displays a listing of all the fonts that are available for the current printer. In step 2, you select one of the fonts by moving the the highlight to it and pressing the Enter key. This returns you to the Document screen where you can see the change in the initial font.

When you use a dot-matrix printer, the size of the font is usually expressed in the number of characters per inch, or *cpi*. In figure 3-5, for example, you can see that most of the font selections have a size ranging from 5 cpi to 20 cpi. The ones that don't have a specific size have an implied size, and they are likely to have a varying number of characters per inch. For business documents, a font at either 10 or 12 characters per inch is

**The soft page break
[SPg]**

> have created with Tabs if I had been using 5.0. Although I'm
> still learning how to use the Tables feature, I finished this
> table in about five minutes.
>
>   Since a table like this used to take me about 20 minutes to
> create, I saved about 15 minutes on this table alone. If I'm
> right, converting to release 5.1 should save our editors about
> five to 20 minutes per table, depending on whether they are
> creating or editing the table. Since we need to create and edit
> many tables, I think converting to release 5.1 will save our
> editors time that is measurable in hours, not minutes.
>
> `The cost of converting to 5.1` The cost of upgrading to 5.1 will
> be about $85 per editor. In addition, the cost of converting from
> 5.0 to 5.1 includes the time it will take our editors to learn how
> to use the Tables feature. However, I think our editors can
> quickly learn how to use the Tables feature. In my opinion, the
> --
> hard part of learning the Tables feature is learning how to use
> the math functions to calculate data for each cell. Since our
> editors don't need to calculate any data, it shouldn't take an
> editor more than an hour to learn how to use Tables. The other
> day, for example, I showed Monica how to use Tables. After about
> 45 minutes of learning how to use the feature, she created her
> `D:\LWPDOCS\51REPORT`   `Doc 1 Pg 1 Ln 50 Pos` `18`

**The hard page break
[HPg]**

> have created with Tabs if I had been using 5.0. Although I'm
> still learning how to use the Tables feature, I finished this
> table in about five minutes.
>
>   Since a table like this used to take me about 20 minutes to
> create, I saved about 15 minutes on this table alone. If I'm
> right, converting to release 5.1 should save our editors about
> five to 20 minutes per table, depending on whether they are
> creating or editing the table. Since we need to create and edit
> many tables, I think converting to release 5.1 will save our
> editors time that is measurable in hours, not minutes.
>
> ==
> `The cost of converting to 5.1` The cost of upgrading to 5.1 will
> be about $85 per editor. In addition, the cost of converting from
> 5.0 to 5.1 includes the time it will take our editors to learn how
> to use the Tables feature. However, I think our editors can
> quickly learn how to use the Tables feature. In my opinion, the
> hard part of learning the Tables feature is learning how to use
> the math functions to calculate data for each cell. Since our
> editors don't need to calculate any data, it shouldn't take an
> editor more than an hour to learn how to use Tables. The other
> day, for example, I showed Monica how to use Tables. After about
> `D:\LWPDOCS\51REPORT`   `Doc 1 Pg 2 Ln 3 Pos` `18`

Figure 3-3   How soft and hard page breaks are shown on the Edit screen

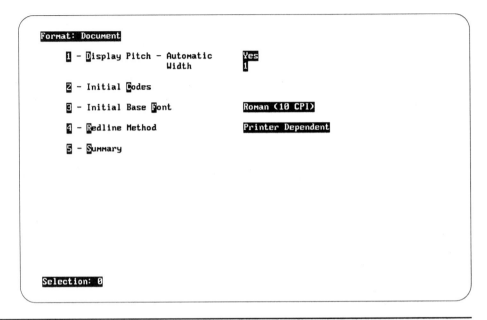

Figure 3-4   The Document screen of the Format command

appropriate. However, because a font at 12 cpi is usually easier to read than a font at 10 cpi, I recommend a 12 cpi font.

To change the initial base font for a document when you're using a laser printer or a dot-matrix printer with *scalable fonts*, the procedure can be a bit more complicated as summarized in figure 3-6. In step 1, you access the Initial Base Font option of the Format command. This displays a listing of all the fonts that are available for the current printer. In step 2, you select one of the fonts by moving the highlight to it and pressing the Enter key.

When the current printer is a laser printer or a dot-matrix printer with scalable fonts, the size of the font is usually expressed in *points* with 72 points to the vertical inch. For most business documents, a size from 10 through 12 points is appropriate. If a font isn't scalable, the size of the type is given right after it in points as in this example:

Times Roman 12pt

Then, when you select the font and press the Enter key in step 2 of the procedure in figure 3-6, *WordPerfect* returns you to the Document screen where you can see the change in the initial font. That ends the procedure.

If the font is scalable, though, no size is given after it as illustrated by the fonts in the screen in figure 3-6. Then, when you select a font in step 2, *WordPerfect* displays this message:

Point size:

The Initial Font screen

```
Document: Initial Font

  Roman ( 5 CPI)
  Roman ( 6 CPI)
  Roman ( 7 CPI)
  Roman (10 CPI)
* Roman (12 CPI)
  Roman (15 CPI)
  Roman (17 CPI)
  Roman (20 CPI)
  Roman 12pt (PS)
  Roman 12pt (PS) Condensed
  Roman 12pt (PS) Dbl-Wide
  Roman 12pt (PS) Italic
  Roman Italic ( 5 CPI)
  Roman Italic ( 6 CPI)
  Roman Italic ( 7 CPI)
  Roman Italic (10 CPI)
  Roman Italic (12 CPI)
  Roman Italic (15 CPI)
  Roman Italic (17 CPI)
  Roman Italic (20 CPI)
  San Serif ( 5 CPI)

 1 Select; N Name search: 1
```

How to change the Initial Base Font

1. Access the Initial Font screen through the Format command (Shift+F8) like this:

   WordPerfect 5.0:   Format > Document > Initial Font
   WordPerfect 5.1:   Format > Document > Initial Base Font

   This displays a screen like the one above.

2. Move the cursor to the font you want to use. When you press the Enter key, *WordPerfect* returns you to the Document screen where you can see the change in the initial font.

   Note: If you're using *WordPerfect* 5.1, you can also use Initial Codes to set the initial font. If you do, the font specified by Initial Codes overrides the font specified by Initial Font.

Figure 3-5   How to change the Initial Base Font for a document when you use a printer without scalable fonts

Here, you type the size that you want for the initial font and press the Enter key as described in step 3. That ends the procedure.

How to set the Initial Codes for a document   To change the default settings for a new document, you can use the Initial Codes option of the Document screen as summarized in figure 3-7. When you access this option, a screen like the one in this figure is displayed. If nothing is shown below the separating line in the middle of the screen, all of *WordPerfect*'s defaults for the initial codes remain in effect. However, if there are codes below the line, someone has changed *WordPerfect*'s defaults. As a result, the codes below the line override the original default settings that came with *WordPerfect*. In this example, the second and third codes override the justification setting and the left and right margin settings.

To add a code to those shown below the line when you're at the Initial Codes screen, you access the Format command again as indicated by step 2 in the procedure in figure 3-7. I know that isn't logical since you've just accessed the Format command to get to the Initial Codes screen option, but that's the way this works. To change the left and right margins, for example, you access the Format command while you're at the Initial Codes screen. Then, you select Line from the Format screen and Margins from the Line screen. After you change the margin settings, you press the Exit key to return to the Initial Codes screen (which means you're still using the original Format command). You will then see the code for the margin settings below the line in the center of the screen. To change any of the other Format options for the document, you proceed in the same way.

If the Initial Codes screen doesn't have a code for justification, you should add one. As I said in the last unit, ragged-right documents are easier to read than justified documents. As a result, the Justification option of the Line screen should be set to Off for *WordPerfect* 5.0 and to Left for *WordPerfect* 5.1.

If the Initial Codes screen doesn't have a code for the Left and Right margins, you should probably add one also. As I said in the last unit, you should try to keep the number of characters in each line of a report to 66 or fewer because that makes the document easier to read. As a result, if you're using a font of 12 cpi or more or a font of 12 points or fewer, you should set larger margins than the one-inch defaults that *WordPerfect* provides. For fonts that are measured in points, you may have to count the number of characters in a line or two of a document to figure out how many characters the average line contains. Then, you can figure out how wide the margins should be.

If you decide that you want to delete one of the codes below the line of the Initial Codes screen, you move the cursor to the code and press the Delete key as described in step 3 of the procedure in figure 3-7. This returns that setting to the original *WordPerfect* default setting. If, for example, you don't want left and right margins of 1.5 inches as shown in the Initial Codes screen in figure 3-7, you move the cursor to this code and press the Delete key. This returns the margins to the *WordPerfect* defaults of one inch. Then, if

The Initial Font screen

```
Document: Initial Font
* ITC Avant Garde Gothic Book Oblique
  ITC Avant Garde Gothic Demi
  ITC Avant Garde Gothic Demi Oblique
  ITC Bookman Demi
  ITC Bookman Demi Italic
  ITC Bookman Light
  ITC Bookman Light Italic
  ITC Zapf Chancery Medium Italic
  New Century Schoolbook
  New Century Schoolbook Bold
  New Century Schoolbook Bold Italic
  New Century Schoolbook Italic
  Palatino
  Palatino Bold
  Palatino Bold Italic
  Palatino Italic
  Symbol
  Times Roman
  Times Roman Bold
  Times Roman Bold Italic
  Times Roman Italic

Point size: 12
```

How to change the Initial Base Font

1. Access the Initial Font screen through the Format command (Shift+F8) like this:

   WordPerfect 5.0:   Format > Document > Initial Font
   WordPerfect 5.1:   Format > Document > Initial Base Font

   This displays a screen like the one above.

2. Move the cursor to the font you want to use and press the Enter key. If the font isn't scalable, *WordPerfect* returns you to the Document screen where you can see the change in the initial font.

3. If you select a scalable font, a prompt like this appears:

   Point size:

   Type the point size that you want to use. When you press the Enter key, *WordPerfect* returns you to the Document screen where you can see the change in the initial font.

Note: If you're using *WordPerfect* 5.1, you can also use Initial Codes to set the initial font. If you do, the font specified by Initial Codes overrides the font specified by Initial Font.

Figure 3-6   How to change the Initial Font for a document when you use a printer with scalable fonts

necessary, you can add another code to replace the one you've deleted. If you see two codes for the same option on the Initial Codes screen, the last one on the screen is the one that's in force.

In figure 3-7, you should delete the first code on the Initial Codes screen. This code sets the initial font for the document, and it takes precedence over the Initial Base Font code. As a result, you should delete the font code on the Initial Codes screen if you want the Initial Base Font code to be in force. (If you're using *WordPerfect* 5.0, you can't use the Initial Codes screen to set the initial font so you don't have to worry about this.)

When you've got the initial codes the way you want them, you press the Exit key to return to the Document options menu. And you press the Exit key again to return to the Edit screen. Then, you can start preparing the document with the knowledge that the initial base font and the formatting codes are set the way you want them.

Later, if you want to change one of the codes for the entire document, you can access the Format command again, select the Document options, and change the codes just as though you hadn't started work on the document. This applies the codes to the entire document without inserting them into the document.

If this seems like a cumbersome way to set the formatting options for a document, it is. Why then should you bother to use Initial Codes and Initial Base Font instead of inserting the formatting codes into the document? First, if you use the Document options, you don't have to worry about putting the codes in the wrong place in the document or about deleting them accidentally. Second, it's sometimes easier to change the default formats by using the Initial Codes screen than it is to insert overriding codes. For example, if you want to return to *WordPerfect*'s default setting, you just delete the code that you don't want. Third, if you combine two or more documents with inserted codes that conflict, you have to find and delete the codes that you don't want. In contrast, if you combine two or more documents that have used the Document options, the second document just assumes the codes of the first one.

How to use the Format command to create a header for a document

If you look at the report in figure 3-1, you'll see the date, file name, and page number at top of each page. This information comes from the *header* for the document. Although you enter a header only once, it prints automatically on each page of the document.

The first procedure in figure 3-8 shows you how to create a simple header that prints on every page of a document. In step 1, you move the cursor to the top of the first page of the document that you want the header to be printed on. If you want the header to start on the first page, the cursor must be at the top of the document before any text. However, the cursor should be

The Initial Codes screen

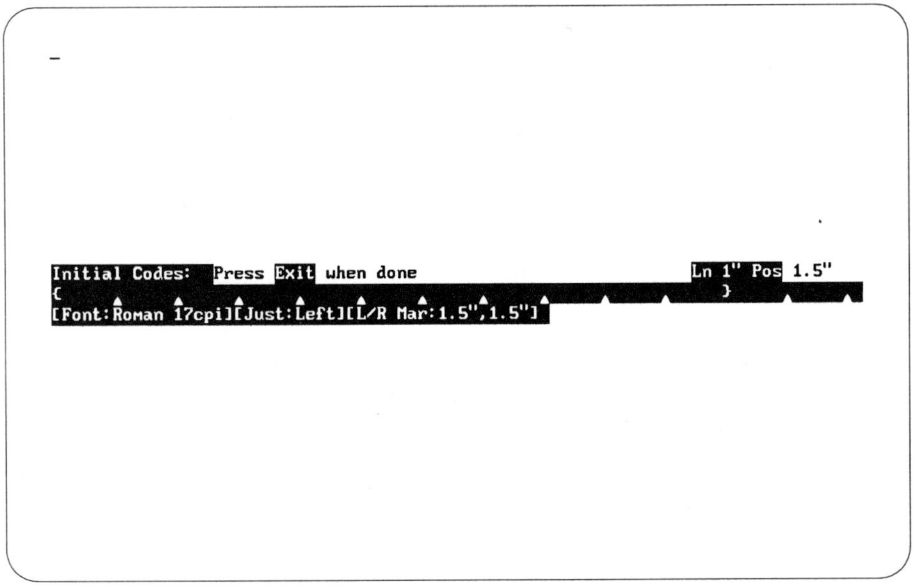

```
Initial Codes: Press Exit when done                    Ln 1" Pos 1.5"
{                                                              }
[Font:Roman 17cpi][Just:Left][L/R Mar:1.5",1.5"]
```

How to change the Initial Codes

1. Access the Initial Codes screen through the Format command (Shift+F8) like this:

   Format > Document > Initial Codes

2. Access the Format command again. Then, use the Line and Page options to set any formatting codes.
3. Use the Delete key to delete any codes.
4. Press the Exit key to return to the Initial Codes screen.
5. Press the Exit key to return to the Document screen.
6. Press the Exit key again to return to the Edit screen.

Figure 3-7   How to change the Initial Codes for a document without inserting codes into the document

after any formatting codes that apply to the header as well as to the rest of the document.

In step 2, you access the Format command and select the Page option. Then, the Page screen is displayed. In steps 3 through 5, you select the appropriate options from the prompts that are displayed: Headers from the

Page screen; Header A from the next prompt; and Every Page from the next prompt. At that point, a Header screen like the first one in figure 3-9 is displayed, and the Edit screen disappears. Then, in step 6, you type the header. In step 7, you press the Exit key (F7) twice: once to exit from the Header screen; once to exit from the Format command.

The Header shown in figure 3-9 is for the report in figure 3-1. When you reach the Header screen, you type the text that you want to be printed at the top of every page of the document. This header can be one or more lines, but one line is often all that you need. *WordPerfect* automatically skips one line between the header and the first line of text as shown in figure 3-1. If you want more than one line skipped, type your header and then press the Enter key once for each extra line that you want skipped between the header and the text.

When you complete the procedure for creating a header, *WordPerfect* inserts a header code into the document at the cursor location. Depending on which release of *WordPerfect* you're using, the code will look like one of these:

[Header A; Every page; ...] or [Header A;2; ...]

If you find a mistake in the header or you want to modify it for some other reason, you can delete the header code and create a new header. Or you can correct the header by using the editing procedure in figure 3-8. As you can see, the procedure for editing a header is similar to the procedure for creating one. When you edit a header, however, the cursor doesn't have to be in any specific location. And you select the Edit option from the second prompt instead of the Every Page option.

The second screen in figure 3-9 shows the Header screen with the codes revealed. The first code inserts the current date. You should remember this code from the last unit. The second code centers the file name, and the third code aligns the page number flush with the right margin. Now, I'll show you how to use the Center and Flush Right commands for your headers.

How to use the Center command

If you look at the command template, you'll see that you access the Center command using the Shift+F6 key combination. To center text as you enter it, you first access the command. This jumps the cursor to the center of the line. Then, you type the text that you want centered. As you type, the characters are centered automatically. Normally, you end the centering function by pressing the Enter key to move to the next line of the document. To center an existing line of text, you move the cursor to the start of the line and access the Center command. *WordPerfect* then automatically centers the line.

How to create a header

1. Move the cursor to the top of the document before any text but after any formatting codes that affect the header.
2. Access the Format command (Shift+F8) and select the Page option.
3. Select the Headers option from the Page screen to display this prompt:

   `1 Header A; 2 Header B: 0`

4. Select Header A.
5. Select the Every Page option from the next prompt:

   `1 Discontinue; 2 Every Page; 3 Odd Pages; 4 Even Pages; 5 Edit: 0`

6. At the Header screen, type a header like the one in figure 3-9; it's the header for the report in figure 3-1.
7. After you enter the header, press the Exit key twice to return to the Edit screen.

How to edit a header

1. From anywhere in your document, access the Format command (Shift+F8) and select the Page option.
2. At the Page screen, select the Headers option to display this prompt:

   `1 Header A; 2 Header B: 0`

3. Select Header A.
4. Then, select the Edit option at the next prompt:

   `1 Discontinue; 2 Every Page; 3 Odd Pages; 4 Even Pages; 5 Edit: 0`

5. Edit the header. Then, when you're done, press the Exit key twice to return to the Edit screen.

Figure 3-8   How to create and edit a header that prints on each page of the document

If you look at the Header screen in figure 3-9, you can see that the file name, 51REPORT, is centered. If you look at the Reveal Codes portion of this screen, you can see that a Center code

[Center]

precedes the file name. Note in this example that the centered text isn't the only text on the line. In fact, it is preceded by the date and followed by the page number.

If you're using release 5.0, your Center code will be different. In this release, the Center command uses two codes if the centered text is followed by any other keystroke. If you typed the header in figure 3-9 using release 5.0, this is what the codes look like:

[Cntr] [C/A/Flrt]

The first code is placed at the beginning of the centered text, and the second code is placed at the end of the text. Although there are these slight differences between the 5.0 and 5.1 codes, the Center command works the same for both releases.

How to use the Flush Right command

If you look at the command template, you'll see that you access the Flush Right command using the Alt+F6 key combination. To right align text as you enter it, you access this command. This jumps the cursor to the right side of the line. Then, you type the text that you want aligned. To end this function, you press the Enter key to move to the next line of the document.

To right align text after you have entered it, you move the cursor to the start of the text that you want right aligned. Then, you access the Flush Right command. When you move the cursor to the next line of the document, the text is aligned on the right margin.

In figure 3-9, you can see that the page number is right aligned. If you look at the Reveal Codes portion of this screen, you can see that the page number is preceded by the Flush Right code:

[Flsh Rgt]

Like the Center code, *WordPerfect* 5.0 uses two Flush Right codes if the text that is right aligned is followed by any other keystrokes. But again, the differences between the release 5.0 and 5.1 codes are trivial; they don't affect the way the Flush Right command works.

How to use the Search command

If you look at the command template, you can see that it includes two Search commands: >Search and <Search. You can use these commands to search for a string of letters, numbers, characters, or codes in your document. A *forward search* (F2) searches from the cursor to the end of a document. A *backward search* (Shift+F2) searches from the cursor to the start of the document.

Figure 3-10 shows you how to use the Search command. In step 1, you move the cursor to where you want the search to begin. In step 2, you access the appropriate Search command. *WordPerfect* then displays a prompt that asks you to enter a *search string* that contains the characters and codes that you want to search for. In step 3, you enter that search string. In step 4, you press the F2 key again, not the Enter key, to start the search. If you press the Enter key, you enter a hard return [HRt] into the search string.

In figure 3-10, you can also see some typical search strings. If, for example, you want to search for the word *analysis*, you just type it in. If you want to search for words that are boldfaced, you press the F6 key to enter the Bold code as the search string. If you want to search for the ends of paragraphs, you press the Enter key twice to enter the hard return codes.

The Header screen

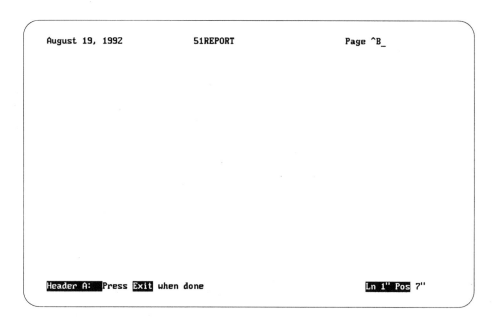

The same screen with the codes revealed

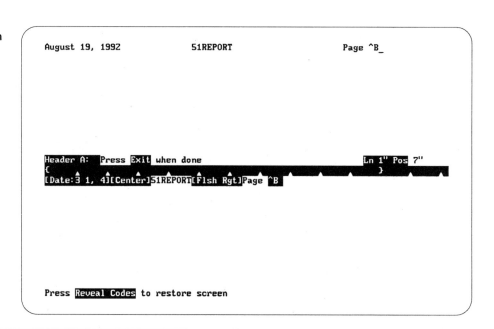

Figure 3-9   The Header screen for release 5.1 after a header has been entered into it

To find all occurrences of a word like *analysis*, you type it in lowercase letters as shown in figure 3-10. Then, *WordPerfect* finds the word whether or not any of its letters are capitalized. In contrast, if you type the word in the search string with any capital letters, *WordPerfect* will find the word only if it's capitalized exactly the same way as it is in the search string.

When the search starts, *WordPerfect* searches for the first occurrence of the search string. If it finds one, it moves the cursor to the end of that occurrence. Then, if you want to search for the next occurrence of the search string, you start the forward or backward search again by pressing F2 or Shift+F2 twice. The first time you press it, the search string is displayed again; the second time you press it, the search begins. You can continue in this way until *WordPerfect* has found all of the occurrences of the search string. When *WordPerfect* can't find another occurrence, it flashes this message

* Not Found *

and leaves the cursor where it was when the search began.

When you use the Search command, you'll find that you often need to limit your search by making the search string more specific. For instance, if your search string is *one*, *WordPerfect* will also find the words *bone*, *none*, and *alone*. So if you want to limit your search to the word *one*, you can put one space before the word when you enter it in the search string.

Often, you can use spaces to limit a search as shown in the last two examples in figure 3-10. Even though you can't see the spaces when you type them in the search string, *WordPerfect* recognizes them. You can also use codes, punctuation marks, and capitalization in a search string to limit a search.

If you decide to change a search string, you press the F2 key once to display the previous search string. Then, if you want to replace the old search string, you just enter the new string. However, if you want to modify the old search string, you can use the Arrow keys, the Backspace and Delete keys, and insert and typeover modes to edit the old string.

There are several ways that you can use the Search command to improve your efficiency as you edit a document. For instance, you can use the Search command to move the cursor to where you want to begin editing. You can use the command to search for a frequently misused word like *it's* to make sure that you used the word correctly. You can use the command to search for terms to make sure that you used them consistently. And you can use the command to search for codes within the document to make sure that your formatting was consistent.

How to use the Replace command

Once you know how to use the Search command, you won't have any trouble using the Replace command. This command searches for a search string just like the Search command, but when it finds an occurrence of the search

How to search for a search string

1. Move the cursor to where you want to begin the search.
2. Access the appropriate Search command. If you want to search forward, press F2. If you want to search backward, press Shift+F2.
3. Enter the search string at the prompt:

   >Srch: (prompt for a forward search)

   <Srch: (prompt for a backward search)

   Note: An arrow appears before the prompt to tell you which direction the search will proceed.

4. After you enter the string, press the F2 key (not the Enter key) to start the search. If *WordPerfect* finds a sequence of characters that matches the search string, it stops the cursor at the end of the matching string. If *WordPerfect* doesn't find a match, it briefly displays this message

   * Not Found *

   and ends the search.

Some typical search strings

>Srch: analysis
<Srch: [Bold]
<Srch: [HRt][HRt]
>Srch: one
>Srch: [sp]one   (where [sp] equals one space)
>Srch: .[sp][sp]   (where [sp] equals one space)

Figure 3-10   How to use the Search command

string, it replaces that string with the *replace string* that you've entered. Because the Replace command is closely related to the Search command, it's sometimes referred to as the Search and Replace command.

If you look at the command template, you'll see that you access the Replace command using the Alt+F2 key combination. Figure 3-11 shows you how to use this command. In step 1, you move the cursor to where you want the replace function to start. Usually, this is at the beginning of a document. When you start the Replace command in step 2, *WordPerfect* displays this prompt:

w/Confirm? No (Yes)

Then, you select No if you're sure that you to want to replace every occurrence of the search string with the replace string. If you're not sure, you select Yes. Then, *WordPerfect* gives you a chance to either skip each occurrence or to replace it with the replace string. In steps 3, and 4, you enter the search string for the function followed by the replace string.

When the Replace function starts, it searches for the first occurrence of the search string. If you selected Yes in step 2 to confirm each replacement, *WordPerfect* displays a prompt like this:

Confirm? No (Yes)

If you select Yes, the first occurrence of the search string is replaced by the replace string, and *WordPerfect* looks for the next occurrence of the search string. If you select No, that occurrence of the search string will be left as it is and *WordPerfect* will continue to search for the next occurrence.

If you selected No in step 2 to indicate that you don't want to confirm each replacement, the Replace command automatically replaces every occurrence of the search string with the replace string without any prompting. In this case, the function can be called a *global replace*.

Because a global replace function can drastically change a document in just a few seconds, here are two precautions you can take when you use it. First, you can save your document before you execute the global replace. Then, if the global replace function doesn't work quite the way you want it to, you can clear the screen, retrieve the old document, and try it again. Second, you can try the search string that you're going to use in a Search command before you try it in the Replace command. That way, you can be sure that the search string is only going to find what you want it to.

Like the Search command, the Replace command can help you edit more efficiently. For instance, you can search for the numbers 1 through 10 and replace them with their spelled-out form (a common editorial standard) as shown in the first example in figure 3-11. You can search for the word *which* and replace it with the word *that* (whenever *that* is appropriate) to make your writing less formal as shown in the second example. If you've been writing about *WordPerfect* and have been spelling it without capitalizing the letter *p*, you can search for *wordperfect* and replace it with *WordPerfect* as shown in the third example. If you decide that you want to underline all occurrences of *WordPerfect* because it is a product name, you can do that as shown in the fourth example. If you decide that you want to indent all paragraphs, you can do that as shown in the fifth example. And if you decide that you don't want to use boldfacing to emphasize words, you can remove the boldfacing by replacing the boldface codes with nothing as shown in the sixth example.

How to replace text with other text

1. Move the cursor above any text that you want to replace. (Unlike the Search command, the Replace command only searches forward.)
2. Access the Replace command (Alt+F2) and select a confirm option at this prompt:

   `w/Confirm? No (Yes)`

   If you want to confirm each replacement, select Yes. If you don't, select No.
3. Enter the search string at this prompt:

   `>Srch:`

   Then, press the F2 key.
4. Enter the replace string at this prompt:

   `Replace with:`

   Then, press the F2 key to start the search and replace function.

Some typical search and replace strings

w/Confirm?	Search string	Replace string
Yes	[sp]5	five
Yes	which	that
No	wordperfect	WordPerfect
No	wordperfect	[UND]WordPerfect[und]
Yes	[HRt][HRt]	[HRt][HRt][Tab]
Yes	[Bold]	

Figure 3-11 How to use the Replace command

How to use the Spell command

You can use *WordPerfect*'s Spell command to check a document for spelling and for certain types of typographical errors. To check for spelling, *WordPerfect* looks up each word in an electronic dictionary of about 115,000 words. If the word is in the dictionary, *WordPerfect* assumes it's correct. If it isn't, *WordPerfect* displays a screen that lets you correct the word. This feature of *WordPerfect* is often referred to as the *spell check feature* or as the *spelling checker*. *WordPerfect*'s spelling checker runs so fast on most PCs that you'll be able to check most documents in less than 30 seconds.

Although the spelling checker usually finds most of the errors in a document, it won't catch all spelling and typographical errors. If, for example, you spell *there* as *their*, the checker won't catch the error because both words are in its dictionary. Similarly, if you type *though* when you mean to type

1. Access the Spell command (Ctrl+F2). Then, *WordPerfect* displays this prompt:

   Check: 1 Word; **2 P**age; **3 D**ocument; **4 N**ew Sup. Dictionary; **5 L**ook up; **6 C**ount: **0**

2. Select the Document option.
3. Respond to the Not Found, Double Word, and Irregular Case screens that *WordPerfect* then displays.

Figure 3-12   How to use the Spell command

through, the checker won't catch the error. Nevertheless, the spelling checker is a useful feature that you should use on just about every document that you create.

Figure 3-12 shows you how to use the Spell command. First, you access the command by pressing the Ctrl+F2 key combination. This displays a prompt with six options, but the first three are the ones you'll use most of the time:

Check: 1 Word; 2 Page; 3 Document

These options let you check the spelling of a single word, a single page, or the entire document.

When you select an option, *WordPerfect* starts the search for errors. Whenever it finds one, it displays a screen with options you can select to correct the error. To correct the errors, you respond to the screens that are displayed.

Both release 5.0 and 5.1 display these two screens: Not Found and Double Word. The Not Found screen indicates a spelling error. The Double Word screen indicates the use of the same word two times in a row (a common typing error). If you're using release 5.1, it also displays a third screen: Irregular Case. This screen indicates that a word is entered in a way that usually isn't correct, like *firSt* instead of *first*.

You can see a typical Not Found screen in figure 3-13. Here, the highlighted word *analisis* is the one that *WordPerfect* couldn't find in its dictionary. Then, just below the horizontal line that divides the screen, *WordPerfect* lists some possible corrections for the word. At the bottom of the screen, *WordPerfect* displays a selection line.

If one of the listed words is correct, type its letter. Then, *WordPerfect* replaces the incorrect word with the word you selected, and it continues the spelling check. If, for example, you press *a* for *analysis*, *WordPerfect* replaces the word *analisis* in the document with the word *analysis*. Since you use letters to select from the list of possible corrections, you must use numbers to select the options from the selection line at the bottom of the screen.

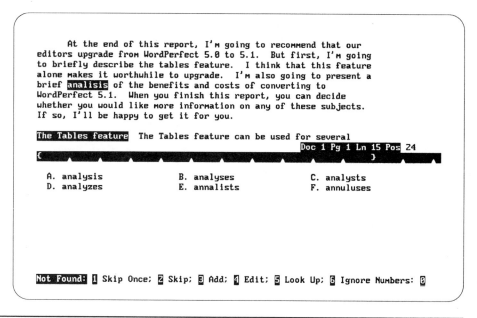

At the end of this report, I'm going to recommend that our editors upgrade from WordPerfect 5.0 to 5.1. But first, I'm going to briefly describe the tables feature. I think that this feature alone makes it worthwhile to upgrade. I'm also going to present a brief `analisis` of the benefits and costs of converting to WordPerfect 5.1. When you finish this report, you can decide whether you would like more information on any of these subjects. If so, I'll be happy to get it for you.

`The Tables feature` The Tables feature can be used for several

Doc 1 Pg 1 Ln 15 Pos 24

| A. analysis | B. analyses | C. analysts |
| D. analyzes | E. annalists | F. annuluses |

`Not Found:` 1 Skip Once; 2 Skip; 3 Add; 4 Edit; 5 Look Up; 6 Ignore Numbers: 0

Figure 3-13   The Not Found screen of the Spell command

If the word that's highlighted is correct, you can press *1* to skip it for this time only or *2* to skip it for the rest of the spelling check. If you want to add the word to the spelling dictionary, you press *3*. If you want to edit the word, you press *4*. This moves the cursor to the word so you can correct it. Then, after you correct it, you press the Enter or Exit key to continue with the spelling check. If the highlighted word consists of a combination of letters and numbers like F3, you can press *6* if you want to ignore words with embedded numbers for the rest of the spelling check.

The Double Word and Irregular Case screens work much like those for the Not Found screen. For a double word, you can press *2* to skip it, *3* to delete the second word, *4* to edit it, or *5* to stop checking for this type of error for the rest of the spelling check.

For an irregular case, you can press *2* to skip it, *3* to replace it, *4* to edit it, or *5* to stop this type of checking. You should be careful how you correct an irregular case, though, because the Replace option doesn't always work the way you would expect. That's why I suggest that you choose the Edit option instead of the Replace option to correct an irregular case. This way, you can make sure that the word is corrected properly.

If you want to cancel the spelling checker at any time during its operation, you can press the Cancel key (F1). When you do, *WordPerfect* displays a message that gives you a count of the number of words that were checked. *WordPerfect* also gives you a word count when the spelling checker is allowed to run to its normal completion. As a result, you can use the spelling checker to count the number of words on a page or the number of words in your whole document. This is useful when you have to keep your document within a certain word count.

How to use the Help command

WordPerfect provides a Help feature that you can use to access much of the information that's in the *WordPerfect* manuals. Since you can access the help information while you're working on a document, this feature is often referred to as *on-line help*.

Figure 3-14 summarizes the main keystroke combinations you need for using the Help feature. To access this feature, you use the Help command (F3). To exit from this feature and return to the Edit screen, you press the Enter key or the Spacebar. This is important to remember because the keys that you usually use to exit from a command (like the Esc, Cancel, or Exit keys) don't work with the Help feature.

When you access Help, a screen is displayed that gives you most of the same information that's in figure 3-14. Then, to display the command template, you can press F3 again. Or to display the help information for a command, you press the keystroke combination that accesses that command. If, for example, you want information on the Spell command, you press Ctrl+F2. Then, *WordPerfect* displays a Help screen like one of the ones shown in figure 3-15. Similarly, if you want to display the information for one of the control keys, you just press that key.

When you get the first Help screen for a command, it is likely to offer options for more information. For instance, the Help screens for the Spell command in figure 3-15 offer six additional options. Then, if you want more information on the Document option, you press *3* or *d*. *WordPerfect* 5.1 then displays the screen shown in figure 3-16. *WordPerfect* 5.0 displays a similar screen.

If you don't know how to access a command or function but you know its name, you can look it up in the Help index. You access the Help index from the main Help screen. To use this index, you press the first letter of the command or function that you want. *WordPerfect* then displays an alphabetic list of the features that begin with that letter. For instance, figure 3-17 shows you the screen that you get if you press the letter *p*. As you can see, if you want to get the information for *Page Break, Hard*, you press the Ctrl+Enter key combination. To see the next screen for the index list, you press the number *1* if you're using *WordPerfect* 5.0 or the letter that you used to access the index if you're using *WordPerfect* 5.1.

As you can see from looking at the screens in figures 3-15 and 3-17, the differences between the Help screens for *WordPerfect* 5.0 and 5.1 are mostly

Keystrokes	Function
How to access and exit from the Help feature	
F3	Accesses the Help feature
Enter or Spacebar	Exits from the Help feature
How to access the Help information that you want	
F3	Displays the *WordPerfect* command template so you can find the keystroke combination for the command that you want to get information about. You shouldn't need to do this unless you don't have a template of your own.
Function or control key	Accesses the screen that explains the related command or function. Often, these screens lead to other screens that present more detailed information.
Any letter	Displays the Help Index, an alphabetic list of the Help topics, for the letter entered. If the list doesn't fit on one screen, you go to the next screen by pressing the letter again (5.1) or the number *1* (5.0).

Figure 3-14   How to access and use the Help feature

cosmetic. For instance, the 5.1 Spell screen is somewhat easier to read than the 5.0 screen. And the columns for the index screens are in a different order.

Although most of the differences between the 5.1 and 5.0 Help features are minor, the 5.1 Help feature does offer one major improvement. It is called *context sensitive help*. This means that you can press the Help key (F3) at any time to get information about the command you're using. If, for example, you are at a Not Found screen for the Spell command, you can press the F3 key to get information about the options for that screen. If you're using *WordPerfect* 5.0, you have to exit from the command before you can access the Help feature and the appropriate Help screen. Unfortunately, the 5.1 Help feature doesn't provide context-sensitive help for all functions. When it does, though, this is a significant improvement over the 5.0 Help feature.

Discussion

You have now been introduced to seven more commands that can be accessed from the command template, and 22 commands in all. If you feel confident about your ability to use those commands, you should be able to create and edit a report like the one in figure 3-1 without any help. But if you have any confusion or doubts, please do the exercises at the end of this unit. They should clear up any doubts that you still have.

As you read this unit, you may have noticed that I didn't present the new commands with as much detail as the commands in the last two units. I did this deliberately to get you to try the commands on your own. If you try them,

The 5.1 Help Screen for the Spell command

```
┌─────────────────────────────────────────────────────────────────────┐
│                                                                       │
│   ▐Speller▌                                                           │
│                                                                       │
│        Helps you check the spelling in your document.  The Speller also checks │
│        capitalization errors and double words.  You can spell-check a word, │
│        page, document, or block of text.                              │
│                                                                       │
│        If you are running WordPerfect from two disk drives, retrieve the │
│        document you want to check, insert the Speller diskette into drive B, │
│        then press Spell.                                              │
│                                                                       │
│        ▐1▌ - ▐W▌ord                                                   │
│                                                                       │
│        ▐2▌ - ▐P▌age                                                   │
│                                                                       │
│        ▐3▌ - ▐D▌ocument                                              │
│                                                                       │
│        ▐4▌ - ▐N▌ew Supplementary Dictionary                          │
│                                                                       │
│        ▐5▌ - ▐L▌ook up                                               │
│                                                                       │
│        ▐6▌ - ▐C▌ount                                                 │
│                                                                       │
│                                                                       │
│   ▐Selection: 0▌                              (Press ENTER to exit Help) │
│                                                                       │
└─────────────────────────────────────────────────────────────────────┘
```

The 5.0 Help Screen for the Spell command

```
┌─────────────────────────────────────────────────────────────────────┐
│                                                                       │
│   ▐Speller▌                                                           │
│                                                                       │
│        Helps you check the spelling in your document as well as look for double │
│        words. You can check a word, page, document, or block of text. │
│                                                                       │
│        ▐Disk Drives:▌ If you are running WordPerfect from disk drives, retrieve │
│            the document you want to check, insert the Speller diskette in drive │
│            B, then press ▐Spell▌.                                     │
│                                                                       │
│        Check the spelling of the current:                            │
│        ▐1▌ ▐W▌ord; ▐2▌ ▐P▌age; ▐3▌ ▐D▌ocument                        │
│                                                                       │
│        You can also choose:                                          │
│        ▐4▌ ▐N▌ew Supplementary Dictionary; ▐5▌ ▐L▌ook up; ▐6▌ ▐C▌ount │
│                                                                       │
│                    ▐Type a menu option for more help: 0▌             │
│                                                                       │
│                                                                       │
│                                                                       │
└─────────────────────────────────────────────────────────────────────┘
```

Figure 3-15   The 5.1 and 5.0 Help screens for the Spell command (Ctrl+F2)

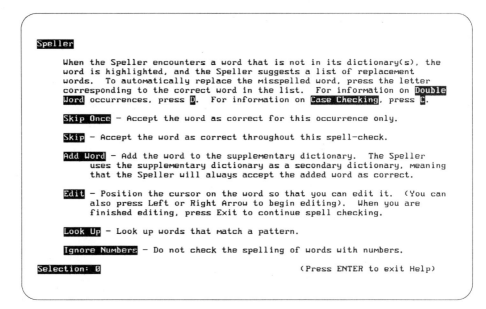

```
Speller

    When the Speller encounters a word that is not in its dictionary(s), the
    word is highlighted, and the Speller suggests a list of replacement
    words.  To automatically replace the misspelled word, press the letter
    corresponding to the correct word in the list.  For information on Double
    Word occurrences, press D.  For information on Case Checking, press C.

    Skip Once - Accept the word as correct for this occurrence only.

    Skip - Accept the word as correct throughout this spell-check.

    Add Word - Add the word to the supplementary dictionary.  The Speller
            uses the supplementary dictionary as a secondary dictionary, meaning
            that the Speller will always accept the added word as correct.

    Edit - Position the cursor on the word so that you can edit it.  (You can
            also press Left or Right Arrow to begin editing).  When you are
            finished editing, press Exit to continue spell checking.

    Look Up - Look up words that match a pattern.

    Ignore Numbers - Do not check the spelling of words with numbers.

Selection: 0                              (Press ENTER to exit Help)
```

Figure 3-16   The 5.1 Help screen for the Spell command after you select Document from the Help screen in figure 3-15

you'll find that they just aren't that difficult to use. Once you know how to access the commands and how to select options from *WordPerfect* prompts, you can learn a lot just by experimenting.

In fact, you can think of your PC with *WordPerfect* running on it as a teaching machine. This machine does whatever you tell it to do. If you use the *WordPerfect* commands correctly, the machine does what you want it to do and positively reinforces your learning. If you use the *WordPerfect* commands incorrectly, the machine doesn't do what you want it to do, and you learn from your mistakes. As a result, all you have to do to keep learning is to keep trying. With this book as a guide, your learning will proceed efficiently because you will be directed to the most essential commands and the most efficient techniques.

As you experiment with *WordPerfect*, you should remember that you can usually recover from a serious error without much trouble. Once you save a document, for example, you can always retrieve it in that earlier form. For that reason, you may want to save your work frequently when you're experimenting with something you haven't used before. Also, remember that you can use the Cancel command to restore (undelete) any one of the last three deletions that you made to a document.

Now that you've completed the tutorial section of this book, you should be able to prepare letters, memos, and reports easily. In fact, you're probably as competent as most *WordPerfect* users in industry.

The 5.1 Help Index

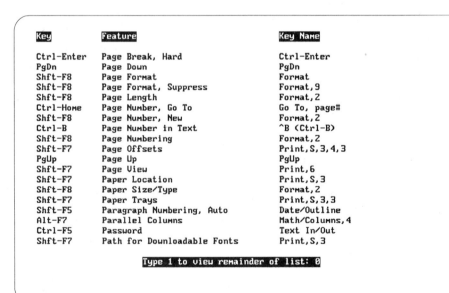

```
Features [P]                      WordPerfect Key   Keystrokes

Page Break, Hard                  Hard Page         Ctrl-Enter
Page Down                         Page Down         PgDn
Page Format                       Format            Shft-F8,2
Page Format, Suppress             Format            Shft-F8,2,8
Page Length                       Format            Shft-F8,2,7
Page Number, Go To                Go To             Ctrl-Home, page#
Page Number in Text               ^B (Ctrl-B)       Ctrl-B
Page Number in Text               Format            Shft-F8,2,6,3
Page Number, New                  Format            Shft-F8,2,6,1
Page Number Style                 Format            Shft-F8,2,6,2
Page Numbering                    Format            Shft-F8,2,6,4
Page Offsets                      Format            Shft-F8,2,7,5,9
Page Up                           Page Up           PgUp
Page View                         Print             Shft-F7,6
Paper Location                    Format            Shft-F8,2,7
Paper Size/Type                   Format            Shft-F8,2,7
Paper Trays                       Print             Shft-F7,s,3,3
Paragraph Down                    Paragraph Down    Ctrl-Down
Paragraph Numbering               Date/Outline      Shft-F5,5
Paragraph Numbering, Auto         Date/Outline      Shft-F5,5
More... Press p to continue.

Selection: 0                                        (Press ENTER to exit Help)
```

The 5.0 Help Index

```
Key          Feature                          Key Name

Ctrl-Enter   Page Break, Hard                 Ctrl-Enter
PgDn         Page Down                        PgDn
Shft-F8      Page Format                      Format
Shft-F8      Page Format, Suppress            Format,9
Shft-F8      Page Length                      Format,2
Ctrl-Home    Page Number, Go To               Go To, page#
Shft-F8      Page Number, New                 Format,2
Ctrl-B       Page Number in Text              ^B (Ctrl-B)
Shft-F8      Page Numbering                   Format,2
Shft-F7      Page Offsets                     Print,S,3,4,3
PgUp         Page Up                          PgUp
Shft-F7      Page View                        Print,6
Shft-F7      Paper Location                   Print,S,3
Shft-F8      Paper Size/Type                  Format,2
Shft-F7      Paper Trays                      Print,S,3,3
Shft-F5      Paragraph Numbering, Auto        Date/Outline
Alt-F7       Parallel Columns                 Math/Columns,4
Ctrl-F5      Password                         Text In/Out
Shft-F7      Path for Downloadable Fonts      Print,S,3

Type 1 to view remainder of list: 0
```

Figure 3-17   The 5.1 and 5.0 Help Index screens for the letter *p*

Terms

hard page break
soft page break
font
base font
initial base font
cpi
scalable font
non-scalable font
point
header
forward search
backward search
search string
replace string
spell check feature
spelling checker
on-line help
context sensitive help

Objectives

1. Use the new commands presented in this unit to perform any of the following functions:

   a) Use the Format command to set the Initial Base Font for a document.
   b) Use the Format command to set the Initial Codes for a document.
   c) Create or edit a header.
   d) Center the text on one line of a document.
   e) Right align the text on one line of a document.
   f) Search any portion of a document, forward or backward, for a given search string.
   g) Replace any occurrences of a search string with a given replace string.
   h) Check the spelling within a document.
   i) Check for double words and irregular cases (5.1) within a document.
   j) Use the help feature of *WordPerfect* 5.0 or 5.1.
   k) Get context sensitive help from *WordPerfect* 5.1.

2. Use any of the skills or commands presented in this unit to create or edit a multi-page document.

Exercises

Part 1: How to use the new commands and keystrokes

1. Start *WordPerfect*. Then, press the F3 key to access the Help feature, and press Ctrl+Enter to get information about hard page breaks. Next, press Ctrl+F2 to get information about the Spell command. Select the Look Up

option on the Spell screen to get information about that option. Is it self explanatory, or would you need information about it before you could use it effectively? To exit from the Help feature, try pressing the Cancel or Esc key. What happens? Now, press the Enter key or the Spacebar to return to the Edit screen.

Access the Help feature again. This time press the letter *s* to get the index for items starting with that letter. Then, find the entry for the Spell command. Note that the index tells you only what keystrokes you need to use (Ctrl+F2) to access the command, and this information is already on the template. Now, press the Enter key to exit from the Help feature.

If you're using *WordPerfect* 5.1, try using the context sensitive help. To do that, access the Format command, select the Page option, and select the Margin option. Then, press the F3 key. Note that the help information for that option is displayed. Next, press the Enter key to exit from the Help feature and then exit from the Format command. Now, see how many keystrokes it takes to access the information on the Page Margins option of the Format command without using context sensitive help. Finally, return to the Edit screen.

2. Your Edit screen should still be blank. Now, access the Print command. Here, in the Select Printer line, you can see the name of the current printer. What is it?

Then, return to the Edit screen. Next, access the Format command and select Document. Here, in the Initial Base Font line (Initial Font line on *WordPerfect* 5.0), you can see the initial base font for the current printer. What is its name and what is its size?

Now, select Initial Base Font. This displays a list of the fonts that are available for the current printer. Are sizes given for these fonts? If sizes are given, are they measured in characters per inch or in points?

Move the highlight to one of the fonts and press the Enter key. If the font isn't scalable, this returns you to the Document screen. But if the font is scalable, *WordPerfect* asks you to enter a type size in points. So type 12 and press the Enter key to return to the Document screen. Here, you can see the initial base font that you've selected for the current document.

3. Assuming that you're still at the Document screen, select Initial Codes. This displays the Initial Codes screen. Are any codes listed below the line in the center of the screen? If so, someone has modified the original *WordPerfect* default settings.

Does one of the codes change the Justification default to ragged right? Whether or not it does, access the Format command, select Line, select Justification, and change the code to Left or Off, depending on which release of *WordPerfect* you're using. Next, while you're still at the Line screen, select Margins and change the left and right margins to 1.5

inches (or 18 units). Then, press the Exit key to return to the Initial Codes screen from the Format command. Here, you can see that Justification and Margin codes have been added to the codes on this screen.

Now, move the cursor to one of the codes on the Initial Codes screen and press the Delete key. This deletes the code. If, for example, there are two codes for the same setting, delete the first of the two codes. Then, make a mental note of the codes that are shown, and press the Exit key to return to the Edit screen.

At this point, you've changed the default settings for the current document, but not for the system. To prove that, use the Exit command to clear the screen and start a new document. Next, access the Format command, and select Document. On this screen, you can see that the Initial Base Font isn't the font that you selected in exercise 2. Instead, it has been returned to its original default setting. Similarly, if you select Initial Codes from the Document screen, you can see that these codes have been returned to their original settings. To end this exercise, press the Exit key twice to return to a blank Edit screen.

4. Your Edit screen should still be blank, and the cursor should be at the top of it. Now, access the Center command, type your name, and press the Enter key. Your name should be centered on the first line of the screen.

Press Home Home Up to move the cursor to the top of the screen. Then, press the Delete key. This deletes the Center code so your name is no longer centered. Next, access the Flush Right command, and press the Down arrow key. Your name should now be right aligned on the first line of the screen.

5. Use the Exit command to clear the Edit screen. Then, use the List command to set the default directory to the one you use for your document files. Next, retrieve the CATLET.FM file that you edited in the last unit. It should look like the one in figure 2-17 except that the date should be the current date.

Use the appropriate Search command to find the word *catalog*. How many times is it used in the letter? Next, use the appropriate Search command to find all occurrences of the Underline code. How many times does the command find this code? Last, use the Search command to search first for the word *I* and then for the word *you*. What search string or strings do you have to use to find each of these words without finding other words?

6. Use the Replace command without the Confirm option to replace all occurrences of the term *PC* with the words *Personal Computer*. Next, use the Replace command with the Confirm option to remove all the Tab codes so the paragraphs in the letter aren't indented. To do that, just

press the F2 key when it's time to enter the replace string. This way, the Tab characters will be removed but not replaced. Last, use the Replace command to replace all occurrences of the letters *sk* with the letters *ks* (this will create some spelling errors for the next exercise).

7. Move the cursor to the start of the word *for* in the first paragraph. Then, insert another word *for* so the spelling checker will find a double word. Next, move the cursor to the first sentence in the second paragraph, and change the word *Least* to *LeaST*.

   Access the Spell command to check the spelling in the letter. When the double word is highlighted, press *3* to delete the extra word. When the first misspelling with *ks* is highlighted, press the letter of the proper replacement word. When the next one is highlighted, press *4* to edit the word. After you correct it, press the Exit or Enter key to continue with the spelling check. If you're using *WordPerfect* 5.1, edit the irregular case when it is highlighted. When all the words have been checked, note the word count of your letter.

   If you're using *WordPerfect 5.0*, the spelling checker didn't recognize *LeaST* as an error. So use the Search command to find it; then, correct it.

8. Move the cursor to the start of the second paragraph. Press Ctrl+Enter to insert a hard page break into the letter. Note that the cursor is below the double line, and note that the page indicator shows page 2. Press the Page-up key to move to page 1 and note the page indicator. Press Ctrl+Home to start the Go-to function. Then, type *2* at the prompt and press the Enter key. This moves the cursor to page 2 again. Although this function isn't useful in a short document like this, you can see that it comes in handy when you work with long documents. Now, with the cursor at the top of page 2, press the Backspace key to delete the hard page break code. If that doesn't work, use the Reveal Codes command so you can be sure to delete the right code. Once it's deleted, note that the entire letter is on one page again.

9. Move the cursor to the start of the second paragraph and press Ctrl+Enter to insert a hard page break into the letter. Next, move the cursor to the start of the second paragraph on the second page and press Ctrl+Enter to create a third page.

   Move the cursor to the top of the first page. Then, use the Format command to create a header for the document. To do that, access the Format command; press *p* for Page; press *h* for Header; press *a* for Header A; and press *p* for Every Page. This should bring you to the Header screen. At that screen, type your name and press the Enter key; type the word *Page* followed by one space; and press Ctrl+B. The left corner of the Header screen should now look like this:

Your Name
Page ^B

Then, press the Exit key twice to exit from the Header screen and from the Format command. When you return to the Edit screen, note that the header doesn't show. Press Reveal Codes, though, so you can see the Header code at the start of the document. Next, return to the normal Edit screen.

Press the Page-down key to move to the second page of the document. Then, edit the header. To do that access the Format command; press *p* for Page; press *h* for Header; press *a* for Header A; and press *e* for Edit. Then, at the Header screen, edit the header so your name and the page number are on the same line with the page number aligned on the right margin of the document.

Now, use the Print command to print all three pages of the document. After the pages are printed, use the Exit command to clear the screen without saving this version of the letter.

Part 2: How to create and edit a report

10. Start with a blank Edit screen. Then, use the Format command to change the Initial Base Font and the Initial Codes for a report like the one in figure 3-1. If, for example, the size of the initial base font isn't 12 cpi or 10 points, select a base font that does have that size. If the justification isn't set for ragged right, change that code so it is. And if the left and right margin settings aren't appropriate for the initial base font you just selected, set them for 1-1/2 inches or the equivalent.

11. Use the Format command to insert a header like the one in figure 3-1. At the Header screen, access the Date/Outline command, and insert a date code at the left margin. Next, access the Center command and type the file name that you're going to use for the report in capital letters. Then, access the Flush Right command and type *Page* followed by one space and Ctrl+B. To finish the header, press the Exit key twice. This should return you to the Edit screen.

12. At this point, type a report. If you're working on a multi-page report of your own, type that report into *WordPerfect*. Otherwise, you can type the report in figure 3-1. Or if you want to save time, just type the first two paragraphs of that report. Then, copy the paragraphs four times each so the paragraphs go beyond the first page of the document.

Whether you type an entire report or just a few paragraphs, type quickly and don't worry about mistakes. Later on, the spelling checker will catch most of them.

As the document goes from the first page to the second page, note the dashed line that indicates a soft page break. Press Reveal Codes so you can see that this line is just a single code [SPg]. Then, press Reveal

Codes again to return to the normal Edit screen.

Now, move the cursor to the top of the last paragraph on the first page and press Ctrl+Enter. This inserts a hard page break [HPg] into the document. As you move the cursor down the second page, note that the soft page break is removed.

Press the Page-up key to move to the top of the first page, and press the Page-down key to move to the top of the second page. Now, press the Backspace key to delete the hard page break. This removes the hard page break and returns the soft page break farther down in the document.

13. Use the Spell command to check the report for spelling errors. Even if you haven't made any mistakes, *WordPerfect* will probably stop at some of the words in the report because they aren't in its dictionary. If these words are okay the way they are, use one of the Skip options to skip them.

14. Use the Print command to print the entire report. Then, use the Page option of the Print command to print just the second page of the report. Next, use the List command to make sure the default directory is the one you're using. And use the Save command to save the report with the file name you used in the heading. Last, use the Exit command to exit from *WordPerfect*.

Section 2

Resource modules

This section contains four independent modules that help you get the most from the tutorial in section 1. If you're already a competent PC user, you probably won't need the first two modules. But if you're new to PCs, these modules provide information that you need for using *WordPerfect* effectively. Module A shows you how to give a legal DOS file specification for a *WordPerfect* file including drive, path, and file name. Module B presents the hardware concepts that you need to understand when you use *WordPerfect*.

Then, module C shows you how to use a mouse and the *WordPerfect* 5.1 menus. Although I don't recommend the use of these menus, most 5.1 users should at least take the time to experiment with them to see if the menus suit their working styles. Last, module D presents a quick summary of the keystrokes and commands that are taught in the tutorial. This summary should be useful to all users of this book because it helps you refresh your memory when you can't quite remember how something you learned earlier works.

Keep in mind that all of the modules in this section are independent. That means you can read or refer to them whenever you need them. You don't have to read them in sequence.

Module A

How to give a file specification when you're using *WordPerfect*

When you want to save or retrieve a document in *WordPerfect*, you need to know the file name. In addition, you often need to know the name of the directory the file is stored in and what drive that directory in is on. In other words, you need to know the complete *file specification* for the document so *WordPerfect* knows exactly where you want to save the document and where to go to retrieve the document after it's saved.

The three parts of a file specification

A complete *file specification* consists of a disk drive, a path and a file name. In figure A-1, for example, you can see complete specifications for a document file on a diskette and for a document file on a hard disk. Now, I'll explain what each part of a file specification is.

The drive   The *drives* on your PC are identified by letters. For example, the first diskette drive on every system is always drive A, and the second diskette drive is always drive B. Similarly, the hard disk (or at least the first portion of it) is always identified as drive C. When you specify the disk drive in a file specification, you always give the drive letter followed by the colon. In figure A-1, you can see that example 1 specifies the A drive, and example 2 specifies the C drive.

However, one hard disk can be divided into more than one drive. For example, figure A-2 shows a hard drive that's divided into two drives. Then, the first portion of the drive is referred to as drive C, the second portion as drive D, and so on. Today, a 40MB drive is likely to be divided into drives C and D, while a 120MB drive is likely to be divided into drives C, D, E, and F.

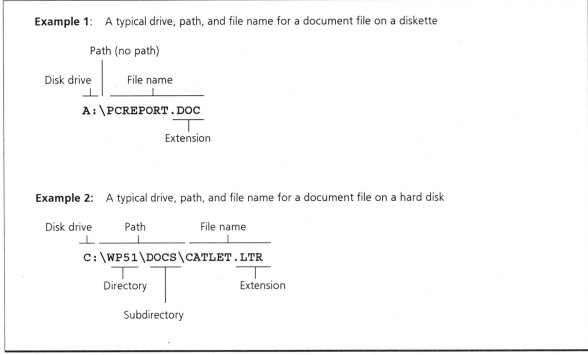

Figure A-1   Typical drives, paths, and file names for document files

The path   The operating system on your PC is called *DOS*. It lets you organize or group files into directories. The 1,368 files on my system, for example, are organized in 39 different directories. These directories are just a special type of file that DOS uses to keep track of the names and locations of the files that are stored on disk. On a DOS system, every file must be stored in a directory.

Figure A-3 illustrates a typical directory structure for a hard disk. For each hard disk or diskette, the top-level directory is always called the *root directory*. In this figure, the root directory contains references to five other directories named DOS, UTIL, WP51, 123, and QA. These directories contain the program files for DOS, for some utility programs, for *WordPerfect* 5.1, for *Lotus 1-2-3*, and for *Q&A*.

Because one directory can contain entries for other directories, the subordinate directories can be referred to as *subdirectories*. In figure A-3, for example, the WP51 directory has two subdirectories named SALES and DOCS while the 123 directory has two subdirectories named SALES and WK1. These subdirectories are just like any other directory; they're just

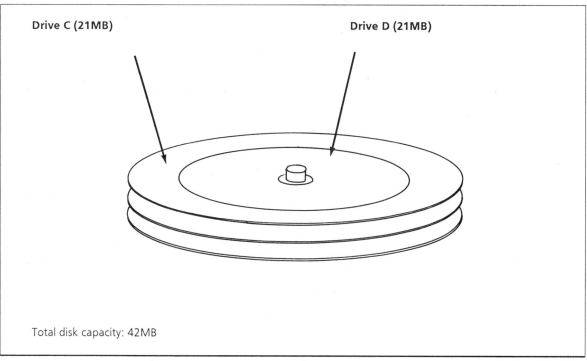

Drive C (21MB)

Drive D (21MB)

Total disk capacity: 42MB

Figure A-2   Two drives on one hard disk

subordinate to a higher-level directory. As a result, subdirectories can also be referred to as directories.

The *path* of a file specification identifies the directory for the file. More specifically, the path tells DOS how to get from the root directory to the directory that contains the entry for the file you want. In the directory structure in figure A-3, the shaded path goes from the root directory to the WP51 directory to the DOCS directory.

Below the directory structure in figure A-3, you can see the specifications for the paths of the eleven directories shown in the structure. The root directory is always specified by the backslash (\). The level-1 directories are identified by the backslash followed by the directory name as in \DOS, \UTIL, \WP51, \123, and \QA. And the level-2 directories, or subdirectories, are identified by the backslash for the root directory, the level-1 directory name, another backslash, and the level-2 directory name as in \WP51\SALES and \WP51\DOCS.

Note in figure A-3 that \DOCS by itself isn't a valid path. To be valid, it must be preceded by its directory as in this path: \WP51\DOCS. Note also

The structure for a set of directories

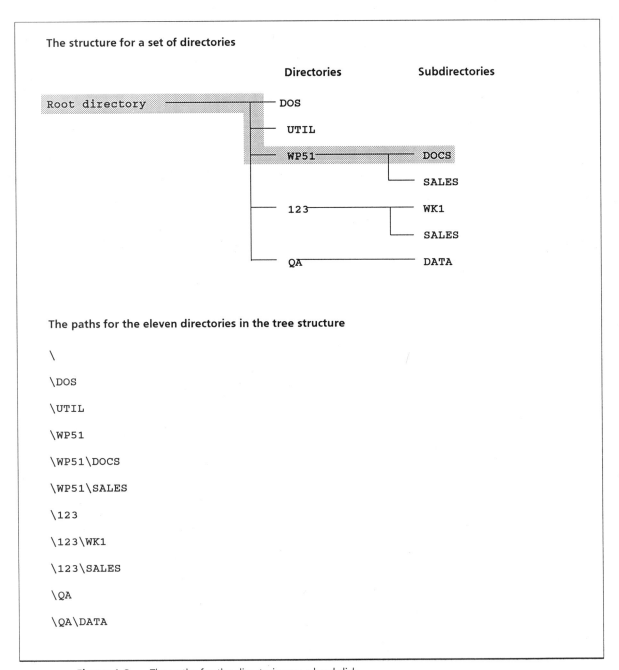

The paths for the eleven directories in the tree structure

\

\DOS

\UTIL

\WP51

\WP51\DOCS

\WP51\SALES

\123

\123\WK1

\123\SALES

\QA

\QA\DATA

Figure A-3   The paths for the directories on a hard disk

that the same subdirectory name can be used within more than one directory. Thus, a SALES directory is subordinate to both the WP51 directory and the 123 directory. To tell them apart, they must be referred to as \WP51\SALES and \123\SALES.

If you look back to figure A-1, you can see that the document file on the diskette doesn't have a path. In general, when you specify a file name for document on a diskette, you just use the drive of the diskette and the file name for the document. Since a diskette can't hold as many files as a hard disk, you usually don't need to use directories to organize the files.

The file name   Whenever you use *WordPerfect* to save a new document file on a hard disk or a diskette, you also need to be able to create a valid *file name*. If you refer back to figure A-1, you can see that a file name is separated into two parts by a period. The part that comes before the period is required. I'll refer to this as the *name* portion of the file name. The part after the period is optional and is called the *extension*.

Figure A-4 gives the rules for forming valid file names. As you can see, you can use from one to eight characters for the name portion and from one to three characters for the extension. This figure also shows the characters that you can't use in a file name.

How to give a file specification when you're using *WordPerfect*

When you use the *WordPerfect* command to list the files in the current directory, it displays a prompt like the one shown in figure A-5. This means that the current *default directory* is:

C:\WP51

As you can see from the prompt, to change the *WordPerfect* default, you can type = and then type the specification for the directory.

When you use the *WordPerfect* Save command, it displays a prompt like the second one shown in figure A-5. If you just enter a file name like PCREPORT at this prompt, the file will be saved in the default directory. If that's not what you want, you can override the default by entering a complete file specification that includes the directory that you want the file saved in. For example, you could type:

D:\WPDOCS\PCREPORT

In this case, the file named PCREPORT is saved in the \WPDOCS directory on the D drive.

When you use the *WordPerfect* Retrieve command, it displays a prompt like the third one shown in figure A-5. If the file you want is in the default directory, you just enter the file name without the extension. Otherwise, you can override the default directory by entering a complete file specification that specifies the drive and directory that you want.

The rules for forming file names

1. The name must consist of from one to eight characters.

2. The extension is optional. If you have one, it must be from one to three characters, and it must be separated from the name by a period as in this example:

    `PCREPORT.DOC`

3. You can use any character in the name or the extension except for the space and any of these characters:

    `. ,   ? / : ; " ' [ ] | \ + = *`

4. You can use either lowercase or uppercase letters in the name or the extension of a file name, but they are treated the same. As a result, the two names that follow are the same:

    `PCREPORT.DOC`   `and`   `pcreport.doc`

Valid file names

`FEB93RPT`

`smith.ltr`

`5-16-93.doc`

`ltr10-21`

`JAN93.WK1`

Invalid file names

`JOHNLETTER.DOC`	(The name is more than 8 characters.)
`JAN:93.WK1`	(The colon is an invalid character.)
`smith.lttr`	(The extension is more than 3 characters.)

Figure A-4   The rules for forming file names

Before you start a *WordPerfect* work session, you should make sure you know what directory you're going to use for your document files. If you're going to put your files in a directory that already exists, you should get the complete specification for that directory. If you're going to put your files in a new directory, you should either make that directory yourself or have someone make it for you. Otherwise, when you go to save your document, you may not save it in the correct directory. Then, you may have a hard time finding it again when you want to edit or print it. Or even worse, you may not be able to find it at all.

The *WordPerfect* prompt for the List command

```
DIR C:\WP51\*.*                    (Type = to change default Dir)
```

The *WordPerfect* prompt for the Save command

```
Name of file to save:
```

The *WordPerfect* prompt for the Retrieve command

```
Name of file to retrieve:
```

Figure A-5   The types of prompts that are displayed by *WordPerfect* when you save or retrieve a document files

Terms

file specification
drive
DOS
root directory
subdirectory
path
file name
extension
default directory

Objectives

1. Given the drive, directory, subdirectory, and name for a file, type a complete file specification

2. Explain how the default directory affects your file specifications when you're using *WordPerfect*.

Hardware concepts and terms for every *WordPerfect* user

Do you know what kind of processor your PC has? Do you know the difference between internal memory and disk storage? And do you know how *WordPerfect* uses internal memory and disk storage for documents?

If you've answered "yes" to all those questions, you can probably skip the material presented in this module. But if you've answered "no" to any of them, you should read this material. To use *WordPerfect* effectively, you need to have a basic understanding of the equipment, or *hardware*, you're using. That's why this module presents the hardware concepts and terms that every *WordPerfect* user should know.

An introduction to PCs

As you probably know, *WordPerfect* is used on *personal computers*, or *PCs*. Today, the term *PC* can be used to refer to the original IBM PC, the IBM PC/XT (or just *XT*), the IBM PC/AT (or just *AT*), and the IBM *PS/2*. The term can also be used to refer to PCs that aren't made by IBM like those made by Compaq, Tandy, and Dell. The PCs that aren't made by IBM are often called *clones* or *compatibles* because they work just like the PCs made by IBM. But it doesn't matter whether you have an XT, an AT, a PS/2, or an IBM compatible. Although the type of PC that you have affects how fast *WordPerfect* runs, it works the same on all PCs.

The physical components of a PC

Figure B-1 shows a typical PC. As you can see, it consists of five physical components: a printer, a monitor, a keyboard, a mouse, and a systems unit. In a laptop PC, the monitor, keyboard, and systems unit are combined into a single carrying case. But on most other systems, these units are separate and

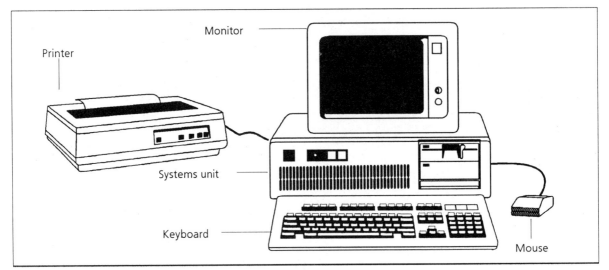

Figure B-1   The physical components of a PC

can be purchased separately. Because you're probably familiar with these five components already, I'll just describe them briefly.

The systems unit   The *systems unit* is the unit that the other physical components are connected to. As you will soon learn, this unit contains the processor that controls the operations of the PC. In contrast to the systems unit, the four other physical components shown in figure B-1 are input and output devices.

The monitor   The *monitor* is an output device. Today, most PCs are sold with *color monitors*. Color monitors can display a variety of colors. *Monochrome monitors*, on the other hand, can display only one color, usually green or amber on a dark background.

Like a television set, a monitor uses dot patterns to display characters and images. The more dots a monitor can display, the higher its *resolution* and the sharper its image. Not surprisingly, high-resolution monitors cost more than low-resolution monitors, just as color monitors cost more than monochrome monitors.

The keyboard   The *keyboard* is the main input device of a PC. Although it resembles the keyboard of a typewriter, a PC keyboard has more keys. The two most common types of PC keyboards: the 84-key and the 101-key keyboards. Although the 84-key keyboard was the original keyboard for the

AT, the 101-key keyboard is now a standard component of all PS/2s and most other PCs.

The mouse   A *mouse* is a small hand-held input device that has two or three buttons on it. If you've ever used a mouse or seen one used, you know that it's just a pointing device. When you move the mouse across a table top (or a *mouse pad* on the table top), a pointer on the monitor moves in the same direction. This pointer on the monitor is called the *mouse cursor*.

With a little practice, you can easily and quickly move the mouse cursor anywhere on the screen. Then, you can *click* or *double-click* the buttons on top of the mouse to perform various actions. If you *click-and-drag* a mouse, you can highlight portions of the screen with the mouse.

The printer   The *printer* of a PC is an output device. Although many different kinds of printers have been developed, the most widely used printers today are dot-matrix printers and laser printers. A *dot-matrix printer* works by striking small pins against an inked ribbon. The resulting dots form characters or graphic images on the paper.

Today, most dot-matrix printers are either 9-pin or 24-pin printers. As you might expect, 24-pin printers print with better quality than 9-pin printers. But both can print text in two different modes: *draft mode* and *letter quality mode*. The draft mode is faster, but the letter quality mode is easier to read.

In contrast to dot-matrix printers, *laser printers* work on the same principle as photocopiers. These printers are not only faster than dot-matrix printers, but they also print with better quality. Today, most laser printers print with 300 dpi (dots per inch), but 1200-dpi printers are also available. Naturally, the print quality (or resolution) of a laser printer depends on the number of dots per inch, and high-resolution printers are more expensive than low-resolution printers.

The primary components of the systems unit

If you've ever opened up the systems unit of a PC, you know that it is full of electronic components. These components are attached to electronic cards that are inserted into the unit. Although you don't have to understand how any of these components work, you should have a conceptual idea of what the primary components of the systems unit are and how they affect the way you use *WordPerfect*.

Figure B-2 is a conceptual drawing of the components of a typical PC. Within the systems unit, you can see four primary components: the diskette drive or drives, the hard disk, internal memory, and the processor.

The diskette drive or drives   A *diskette* is the actual recording medium on which data is stored, and the *diskette drive* is the device that writes data on the diskette and reads data from the diskette. Although diskettes are

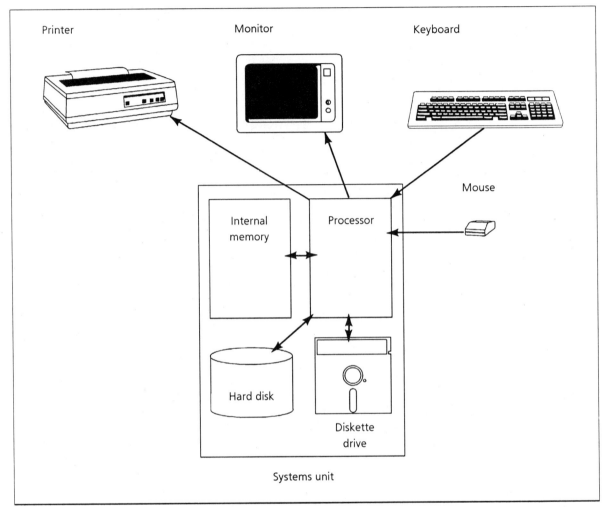

Figure B-2 The internal components of the systems unit

sometimes called *floppy disks*, I'll refer to them as diskettes throughout this book.

To read data from a diskette or write data on a diskette, you insert the diskette into the slot on the diskette drive and close the drive's latch (if it has a latch). If a PC has two diskette drives, they can be in a left and right arrangement, or they can be in a top and bottom arrangement.

There are two sizes of diskettes that can be used with PCs. Originally, all PCs, XTs, and ATs used 5-1/4 inch diskettes, and all PS/2s used the newer 3-1/2 inch diskettes. Today, however, you can install a diskette drive for either type of diskette on an XT, an AT, or a PS/2.

Size	Capacity	Common labelling notation
5-1/4"	360KB	5-1/4" Double-Sided Double-Density 5-1/4" DSDD
5-1/4"	1.2MB	5-1/4" Double-Sided High-Density 5-1/4" DSHD
3-1/2"	720KB	3-1/2" Double-Sided Double-Density 3-1/2" 2DD 3-1/2" 1.0M formatted capacity
3-1/2"	1.44MB	3-1/2" Double-Sided High-Density 3-1/2" 2HD 3-1/2" 2.0M formatted capacity

Figure B-3   A summary of diskette characteristics

To complicate matters, both types of diskettes come in two storage capacities: *standard capacity* and *high capacity*. These capacities are measured in *bytes* of data. For practical purposes, you can think of one byte of data as one character of data, and you can think of a character as a letter, a digit (0-9), or a special character such as #, %, or &. Thus, ten bytes of diskette storage are required to store the word *impossible*; four bytes are required to store the number *4188*; and two bytes are required to store *$9*.

For 5-1/4 inch diskettes, the standard capacity is 360,000 bytes, or 360KB. Here, KB stands for *kilobyte*. One kilobyte is approximately 1,000 bytes. In contrast, the high capacity is 1,200KB, or 1.2MB. Here, MB stands for *megabyte*. One megabyte is approximately one million bytes. For 3-1/2 inch diskettes, the standard capacity is 720KB, and the high capacity is 1.44MB.

Figure B-3 summarizes the diskette sizes and capacities. Because the labelling for diskettes is often confusing, this figure also lists the common labelling designations for each type of diskette. Notice, for example, that the standard capacity diskettes are also called *double density* diskettes, and the high capacity diskettes are also called *high density* diskettes.

The hard disk   In contrast to diskettes, a *hard disk* is installed inside the systems unit. In this case, the recording medium and the drive are sealed together in a single unit. As a result, a hard disk can't be removed from the PC the way a diskette can. That's why hard disks are sometimes called *fixed disks*. In this book, though, I'll only use the term *hard disk*.

Today, most hard disks have capacities of 20MB or more, and you can buy hard disks with capacities of 320MB or more. To put that into perspective, consider that one megabyte of disk storage can hold about 500 pages of word processing text. So a 30MB hard disk can hold 15,000 pages of text, while a 360KB diskette can hold only about 175 pages. To look at it another way, a 40MB disk can store the equivalent of about 110 diskettes that have a capacity of 360KB.

If your PC has a hard disk, you probably won't use diskettes much because all of your programs will be stored on the hard disk. However, you still need at least one diskette drive on your PC. Then, you can use it to back up the data on your hard disk to diskettes, to install new programs from diskettes to your hard disk, and to transfer data from one PC to another.

Internal memory   Before your PC can operate on the data that is stored on a diskette or a hard disk, the data must be read into the *internal memory* of the systems unit. This memory can also be called *internal storage* or *RAM* (for *Random Access Memory*), but I'll refer to it as internal memory throughout this book.

Like diskette or hard disk storage, the capacity of internal memory is measured in kilobytes or megabytes. Although the original PC was typically sold with either 64KB, 128KB, or 256KB of internal memory, a PC today is usually sold with 512KB or 640KB of internal memory. And the newer, more powerful PCs are sold with 1MB, 2MB, or 4MB of internal memory.

The first 640KB of internal memory can be referred to as *conventional memory*. Since the original PC was designed for a maximum memory of 640KB, most programs aren't designed to use more memory than that. But some programs can use either *extended memory* or *expanded memory*. For instance, *WordPerfect* 5.1 can use expanded memory, but not extended memory. However, *WordPerfect* usually works fine on conventional memory alone.

The processor   If you look back to figure B-2, you can see that all of the components I've described so far are connected to the *processor*. When a program is in operation, the processor controls all of the other components of the PC by executing the instructions of the program. Other terms for a processor are *microprocessor*, *central processing unit*, and *CPU*, but I'll use the term *processor*.

Today, PC processors are identified by the *microprocessor chip* they're based on. In an IBM PC or PC compatible, all of the processors are based on chips that were originally manufactured by Intel with names like the 8088, the 80286, and the 80386. These are summarized in figure B-4. As you can see, the shortened versions of the chip names are the 286, the 386SX, the 386, and so on. Because the processor controls all of the operations of a PC, the speed of the processor affects how fast *WordPerfect* runs on your PC.

Processor names	Abbreviated names
8088	None
80286	286
80386SX	386SX
80386DX	386
80486SX	486SX
80486DX	486

Figure B-4   A summary of PC processors

How *WordPerfect* uses internal memory and disk storage

Now that you know what the basic hardware components of a PC are, you should understand how they relate to *WordPerfect*. In particular, you should understand how *WordPerfect* makes use of internal memory and disk storage.

How *WordPerfect* uses internal memory   Part 1 of figure B-5 shows how *WordPerfect* uses conventional memory when it is working on a document. When you start your PC, the operating system (DOS) is loaded into the first portion of internal memory (the first 40KB). Then, when you start *WordPerfect*, it is loaded into the portion of internal memory that follows DOS (from 40KB to 424KB in this example). Next, as you create a document, it is stored in the next portion of internal memory (from 424KB to 560KB in this example). The last portion of memory isn't used so it can be used when you add to the document.

Why you should save a document to disk storage before you exit from *WordPerfect*   Whenever you turn off your PC, the contents of internal memory are lost. Similarly, when you exit improperly from *WordPerfect* and return to the operating system, the document that you've been working on is lost. So if you don't want to lose your work, you must save your document to disk storage on the hard disk or on a diskette before you exit from *WordPerfect* or turn off your PC. Unlike internal memory, the contents of disk storage aren't lost when the PC is turned off.

The process of saving a document to a hard disk is illustrated in figure B-5. In part 1, you can see that the document in internal memory is saved on the hard disk. After the document has been saved, it is still in internal memory, but it is also on the hard disk. After you exit from *WordPerfect*, you can see that neither the program nor the document is in internal memory in part 2. However, the document is still available on the hard disk for use later on.

When you use *WordPerfect*, you are responsible for saving a document to the disk. To do this, you use one of the *WordPerfect* commands called the Save command. Then, the next time you use *WordPerfect*, you can use the List Files screen or the Retrieve command to retrieve the document from disk storage to internal memory so you continue to work on it.

Some perspective on hardware for *WordPerfect* users

Throughout this module, I've tried to simplify the concepts and keep the number of new terms to a minimum. In general, I've tried to present only those PC concepts you need to know in order to use *WordPerfect* effectively. And I've tried to present only those terms that you're most likely to encounter in *WordPerfect* manuals and in magazine articles about *WordPerfect*.

Nevertheless, this module presents more than you need to know about hardware if all you want to do is use *WordPerfect* effectively. As a result, you shouldn't feel that you need to know all of the terms in this module before you continue. The only terms you really should be familiar with are in the list that follows.

Terms you should be familiar with

hardware
personal computer
PC
XT
AT
PS/2
compatible
systems unit
monitor
color monitor
monochrome monitor
keyboard
mouse
mouse cursor
printer
dot-matrix printer
laser printer
diskette
diskette drive
standard capacity
high capacity
byte

kilobyte (KB)
megabyte (MB)
double density
high density
hard disk
internal memory
conventional memory
extended memory
expanded memory
processor
microprocessor chip

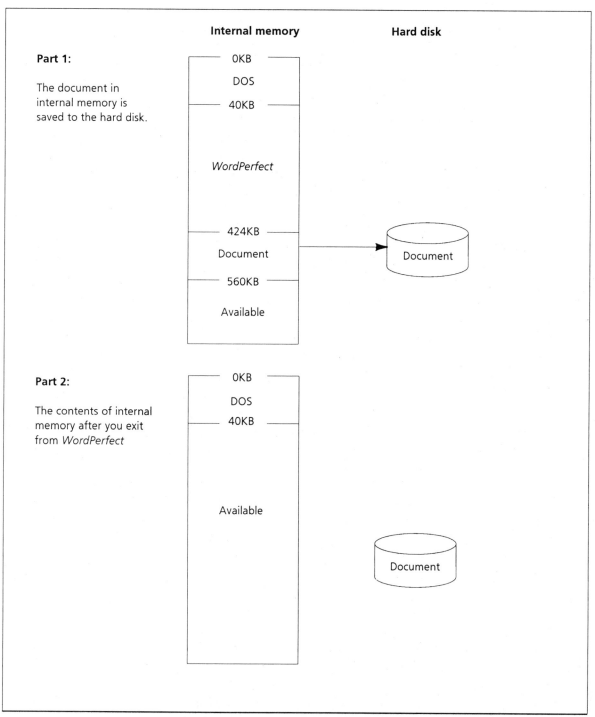

Figure B-5   Why you should save a document to the hard disk before you exit from *WordPerfect*

Objectives

1. List the four primary physical components of a PC.

2. List the four primary components of a systems unit.

3. Explain how *WordPerfect* uses internal memory.

4. Explain why a document should be saved to disk storage before the PC user exits from *WordPerfect* or turns the PC off.

Module C

When and how to use the *WordPerfect* 5.1 pull-down menus

Because I recommend that you use the function keys to access *WordPerfect* screens and commands, this book is designed to be used with the function key interface. However, in *WordPerfect* 5.1, you have the option to use a system of menus, like the menus shown in figure C-1, to access *WordPerfect* screens and commands. In addition, *WordPerfect* 5.1 supports the use of a mouse.

If you want to use the menus, this module will show you how. First, you'll learn how to use the menus with or without a mouse. Then, you'll learn how to set up the menus so you can use them efficiently. Next, you'll learn how to use a mouse with *WordPerfect* screens, selection lines, and prompts. And finally, I'll show you how to use the menus to access the *WordPerfect* screens and commands that are presented in this book. But first, you need to learn some terms that apply to the menu interface.

An introduction to pull-down menus

If you look at figure C-1, you will see several different elements that make up the *WordPerfect* 5.1 menu system. There is a *menu bar* across the top of the screen that has the names of the nine different *WordPerfect* menus on it. These menus are called *pull-down menus* because you pull them down in order to select items from them. In figure C-1, for example, the Font menu is pulled down.

If you look closely at the items on the Font menu, you will see that there is a triangle to the right of the Appearance item. When you select an item with a triangle, *WordPerfect* gives you another menu with more items. Since this menu cascades off to the right side of the pull-down menu, it's called a *cascading menu*. In figure C-1, for example, the Appearance menu cascades off to the right side of the Appearance item on the Font menu. When you select

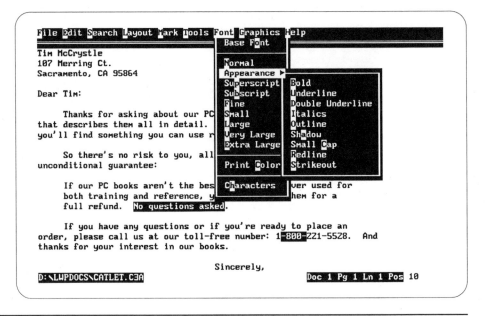

Figure C-1   The pull-down menu for the Font command

an item that doesn't have a triangle, *WordPerfect* executes that item immediately.

As you work with the pull-down menus, you'll realize that they are just another way of doing the same things you can do with the function keys. In other words, there are no additional features that you can use with the menus. And in most cases, the menus lead to the same *WordPerfect* screens, selection lines, and prompts that the function keys lead to.

How to use the pull-down menus

There are three steps to using the menus. First, if the menu bar is not visible, you must display it. Then, you pull down a menu and select an item from it. Figure C-2 shows how to use the menus with a mouse or with the keyboard.

With a mouse   If you are using a mouse, you can display the menu bar by clicking the right button. Then, to pull down the menu you want, move the mouse cursor to that menu and click the left button. To select an item, move the mouse cursor to it and click the left button. If you make a mistake or change your mind, you can back out of the menus by clicking the right button.

With the keyboard   If you're using the keyboard, you can display the menu bar by holding down the Alt key while you press the Equals (=) key.

How to access the menus and items with a mouse

Right button	If you are at the Edit screen, click the right button to display the menu bar.
	If you are in a menu, click the right button to back out of all the menus and return to the Edit screen.
Left button	Move the mouse cursor to an item and click the left button to select it.

How to access the menus and items with the keyboard

Alt key+Equals (=)	Displays the menu bar.
Alt key	Displays the menu bar if you've set this default for your system (figure C-5).
Cursor control keys	Moves the cursor through the menus and items to highlight your selection.
Highlighted letter	Selects the menu or item.
Enter key	Selects a menu item that has been highlighted by the cursor.
Esc key	Backs out of menus one by one. If you are at the menu bar, it returns you to the Edit screen.
Cancel key (F1)	Backs out of menus one by one. If you are at the menu bar, it returns you to the Edit screen.
Exit key (F7)	Backs out of all menus and returns you to the Edit screen.

Figure C-2   How to access the pull-down menus and select items

Then, to pull down the menu you want or to select an item from a menu, you press the highlighted letter of the menu or item. Or you can move the cursor to the menu or item to highlight it, and then press the Enter key. But this method requires more keystrokes, so I don't recommend it. If you make a mistake or change your mind, you can cancel your selection by using the Esc, Cancel, or Exit keys as shown in figure C-2.

How to use a mouse with *WordPerfect* 5.1

If you're used to using a mouse to select items in a WYSIWYG (what-you-see-is-what-you-get) environment, you may find that using a mouse with *WordPerfect* 5.1 is frustrating. That's because *WordPerfect* for DOS wasn't developed with mouse support in mind. Still, if you're used to using a mouse, you may be delighted that you can now use one to block text on the Edit screen and to make selections from *WordPerfect* screens, selection lines, and prompts.

1. Position mouse cursor and hold down the left button.
2. Drag the mouse cursor to the end of the text that you want blocked.
3. Release the left mouse button.

Figure C-3   How to use the mouse to block text

How to block text on the Edit screen

Figure C-3 shows you how to block text on the Edit screen. First, you position the mouse cursor where you want to begin the block. Then, you press and hold down the left mouse button as you drag the mouse cursor to the end of the text that you want to block. This is referred to as the *click-and-drag* technique. To complete marking the block, you release the left mouse button.

How to make selections at the *WordPerfect* 5.1 screens, selection lines, and prompts

Figure C-4 shows you how to use the mouse to make selections at the *WordPerfect* 5.1 screens, selection lines, and prompts. To select an item from a screen or selection line, you move the mouse cursor to the highlighted letter or number of the item. Then, you click the left mouse button.

You can also use the mouse to confirm operations at the prompt line. If, for example, you use the Save command to save an existing document named CATLET in the D:\WPLTRS directory, *WordPerfect* displays this prompt:

Document to be saved: D:\WPLTRS\CATLET

To confirm the save operation, you position the mouse cursor on the prompt and press the right mouse button.

How to set up the pull-down menus so they work the way you want them to

WordPerfect 5.1 gives you several options for setting up the pull-down menus. You set these options at the Menu Option screen shown in figure C-5. To access the Menu Option screen, you pull down the File menu and select Setup. Then, you select Display from the Setup menu. And finally, you select Menu Options from the Display screen. The two most important options on this screen are the Alt-Key-Selects-Pull-Down-Menu option and the Menu-Bar-Remains-Visible option.

The Alt-Key-Selects-Pull-Down-Menu option

If you use the keyboard to select menus, you'll probably want to set this option to Yes. Then, you can display the menu bar by pressing the Alt key. Otherwise, you have to press the Alt+Equals key combination to display the menu bar.

Left button	To select an item, move the mouse cursor to a highlighted number or letter and click the left button.
Right button	To confirm a prompt, position the mouse cursor on the prompt and click the right button.
	To back out of menus, selection lines, or prompts and return to the Edit screen, click the right button.

Figure C-4   How to use the mouse to select, confirm, and exit from screens, selection lines, and prompts

The Menu-Bar-Remains-Visible option   Whether or not you keep the menu bar visible is up to you. If it's visible, you save a keystroke or mouse click every time you want to select a menu. And you might feel more comfortable with the menu bar shown at the top of the screen. On the other hand, when the menu bar is visible, you can't see as many lines of text on the Edit screen.

How to use pull-down menus to access the Format screens

Figure C-6 shows you how to access the Format screen with the pull-down menu system. As you know from units 2 and 3, you use Line options of the Format command to set the justification, left and right margins, and line spacing for a document. And you use the Page options of the Format command to vertically center the text on a page, set the top and bottom margins, and create a header for a document. In addition, you use the Document options of the Format command to set the initial base font for the document and to set initial codes for a document that override pre-set default settings.

How to use pull-down menus to access the *WordPerfect* commands presented in this book

Figure C-7 is an alphabetical list of the *WordPerfect* commands that are presented in this book. So, if you can't figure out how to access a command with the menus, you can use this figure for reference.

Terms   menu bar
pull-down menu
cascading menu

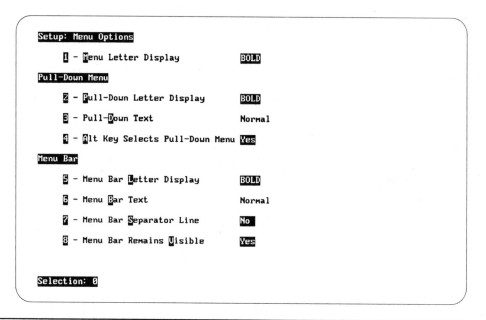

Figure C-5   The Menu Options screen

Format screens	Menu access
Line	Layout > Line
Page	Layout > Page
Document	Layout > Document

Figure C-6   How to use the menus to access the options of the Format screen

Objectives

1. Access the menu bar and select commands using either the mouse or the keyboard.

2. Use the mouse to block a portion of text on the Edit screen.

3. Use the mouse to select options and confirm operations at the *WordPerfect* prompt line.

4. Display the menu bar always by setting the appropriate option.

Command name	Access
Block	Click-and-drag mouse
	Edit > Block
Bold	Font > Appearance > Bold
Cancel	Esc
	Right mouse button
	Edit > Undelete
Center	Layout > Align > Center
Date	Tools > Date Code
	Tools > Date Text
Exit	File > Exit
Flush Right	Layout > Align > Flush Right
Format	Layout> Line
	Layout> Page
	Layout> Document
Help	Help > Help
	Help > Index
	Help > Template
Indent, single	Layout > Align > Indent ->
Indent, double	Layout > Align > Indent -><-
List Files	File > List Files
Move	Edit > Select
	Edit > Move
	Edit > Copy
	Edit > Delete
	Edit > Paste
Print	Edit > Print
Replace	Search > Replace
Retrieve	File > Retrieve
Reveal Codes	Edit > Reveal Codes
Save	File > Save
Search, backward	Search > Backward
Search, forward	Search > Forward
Spell	Tools > Spell
Underline	Font > Appearance > Underline

Figure C-7   An alphabetical listing of the commands presented in this book

Module D

A brief summary of the *WordPerfect* keystrokes and commands presented in this book

This module summarizes the keystrokes and commands that are presented in the tutorial section of this book. Within each summary, the keystrokes and commands are grouped by function. If a command can logically be placed in two or more of these groups, it's placed in all of them. For each command, you are referred to the primary figures in the text that present the command. If there are no figures for the command, however, you are referred to the primary pages in the text that explain the command. Since some commands and keystrokes function differently if text is blocked on the screen, I've presented a summary of commands that you can use on blocked text. Because this module presents the keystrokes and commands in a new order, it can help you review the *WordPerfect* skills presented in the tutorial section of this book.

Keystroke summary

Keystrokes   **Function**

How to move the cursor

The Ctrl key and the Arrow keys

Ctrl+Right   Moves the cursor right one word at a time.
Ctrl+Left   Moves the cursor left one word at a time.

Ctrl+Up (5.1)   Moves the cursor up one paragraph at a time.
Ctrl+Down (5.1)   Moves the cursor down one paragraph at a time.

The Home key and the Arrow keys

Home Left   Moves the cursor to the left of the line after all codes.
Home Right   Moves the cursor to the right of the line after all codes.

Home Up   Moves the cursor to the top of the Edit screen.
Home Down   Moves the cursor to the bottom of the Edit screen.

Home Home Up   Moves the cursor to the top of the document after all codes.
Home Home Down   Moves the cursor to the bottom of the document after all codes.

Home Home Home Up   Moves the cursor to the top of the document before all codes.
Home Home Home Left   Moves the cursor to the left of the line before all codes.

The End key

End   Moves the cursor to the right of the line after all codes.

The Page keys

Page-up   Moves the cursor to the top of the previous page.
Page-down   Moves the cursor to the top of the next page.

The Plus (+) and Minus (-) keys on the numeric pad with Num-lock off

+   Moves the cursor to the bottom of the Edit screen.
-                         Moves the cursor to the top of the Edit screen.

The Go to command

Ctrl+Home   Moves the cursor to the top of the page you specify at the Go to prompt by entering the page number.

How to delete text

Keystrokes	Function
Ctrl+Delete	Deletes the word at the cursor.
Ctrl+Backspace	Deletes the word to the left of the cursor.
Ctrl+End	Deletes from the cursor to the end of the line.
Ctrl+Page-down	Deletes from the cursor to the end of the page.

How to work with pages

Ctrl+Enter	Inserts a hard page break [HPg] into the document.
Ctrl+B	Inserts an automatic page number into the document.

How to move between *WordPerfect* screens

Highlighted letter or number	Selects an option.
Esc	Returns to the previous screen.
Cancel (F1)	Returns to the previous screen.
Zero (0)	Returns to the previous screen.
Exit (F7)	Returns to the Edit screen.

Editing commands

Key name	Function	Refer to figure or page (p)
Block	Turns block on to block if no text is blocked; turns block off if text is already blocked.	2-10
Cancel	Undeletes the blocked text shown on your Edit screen.	2-7
Date/Outline	Automatically types the current date into your document, or inserts a code for the current date.	2-8
Esc	Repeats a function n times	p 56
Format	Accesses the Page options for setting headers, and footers.	2-11, 2-12, 3-8
Move	Moves, copies, or deletes a sentence, paragraph, page, or block.	2-9, 2-10
Replace	Searches for a string of text and replaces that string of text with another string of text.	3-11
Reveal Codes	Toggles between the Edit screen and the Reveal Codes screen.	1-14
<Search	Searches for a string of text from the cursor to the beginning of the document.	3-10
>Search	Searches for a string of text from the cursor to the end of the document.	3-10

Formatting commands

Key name	Function	Refer to figure or page (p)
Bold	Boldfaces text.	p 19, 2-10
Center	Centers text.	p 108-110
Flush Right	Aligns text with right margin.	p 110
Format	Accesses the Line, Page, and Document options for setting margins, line spacing, and so on.	2-12 through 2-14, 3-4 through 3-7
>Indent	Indents a paragraph one tab stop from the left margin.	p 13, p 18-19
>Indent<	Indents a paragraph one tab stop from the left margin and an equal amount from the right margin.	p 18-19
Reveal Codes	Toggles between the Edit screen and the Reveal Codes screen.	1-14
Underline	Underlines text.	p 18-19, 2-10

File handling commands

Exit	Clears the document, *WordPerfect*, or both from internal memory.	1-19
List	Sets the default directory and accesses the List screen.	2-2, 2-3
Retrieve	Retrieves a document from disk into internal memory.	2-4
Save	Saves a document from internal memory to disk.	1-17

Printing commands

Key name	Function	Refer to figure or page (p)
Print	Accesses the Print screen (see Print screen functions).	1-16
List	Accesses the List screen (see the Print option on the List screen options).	2-3

Spelling checker, Thesaurus and Help commands

Spell	Accesses the spelling checker.	3-12, 3-13
Help	Accesses the Help feature.	3-14 through 3-17

Commands that you can use on a block of text

Key Name	Function
Move	Moves or copies a block of text.
Delete	Deletes a block of text.
Print	Prints a block of text.
Save	Saves a block of text to a named file (the default directory is assumed unless you override it by giving a complete file specification).
Spell	Checks the spelling of the words in the block and counts the number of words in the block.
Bold	Boldfaces the blocked text.
Underline	Underlines the blocked text.

Index

Comment Form

Your opinions count

If you have any comments, criticisms, or suggestions for us, I'm eager to get them. Your opinions today will affect our products of tomorrow. And if you find any errors in this book, typographical or otherwise, please point them out so we can correct them in the next printing.

Thanks for your help.

Mike Murach

Book title: The *WordPerfect* Tutorial

Dear Mike: _____

_____

_____

_____

_____

_____

_____

_____

_____

_____

_____

_____

_____

_____

_____

_____

_____

Name_____

Company (if company address) _____

Address _____

City, State, Zip _____

Fold where indicated and tape closed.

No postage necessary if mailed in the U.S.

fold

fold

BUSINESS REPLY MAIL

FIRST-CLASS MAIL   PERMIT NO. 3063   FRESNO, CA

POSTAGE WILL BE PAID BY ADDRESSEE

Mike Murach & Associates, Inc.

4697 W JACQUELYN AVE
FRESNO CA 93722-9888

 Il.l....ll.l...l.l.l..l.ll.l..l.l.l..l.l..l.l.l.ll

fold

fold

Order Form

Our Ironclad Guarantee

To our customers who order directly from us: You must be satisfied. Our books must work for you, or you can send them back for a full refund...no questions asked.

Name & Title _____

Company (if company address) _____

Street address _____

City, State, Zip _____

Phone number (including area code) _____

Fax number (if you fax your order to us)_____

Qty	Product code and title	*Price
WordPerfect		
____ WPTU	The *WordPerfect* Tutorial	$10.00
____ LWP	The Least You Need to Know about *WordPerfect*	20.00
Lotus 1-2-3		
____ LLOT	The Least You Need to Know about *Lotus 1-2-3*	$20.00
____ GLOT	The Practical Guide to *Lotus 1-2-3*	25.00

Qty	Product code and title	*Price
Introduction to Microcomputing		
____ DWPL	DOS, *WordPerfect*, and *Lotus* Essentials	$25.00
DOS		
____ LDOS	The Least You Need to Know about DOS	$17.95
____ LDS2**	The Least You Need to Know about DOS (2nd Ed.)	20.00
____ DOSB	The Only DOS Book You'll Ever Need	24.95
____ DOS2**	The Only DOS Book You'll Ever Need (2nd Ed.)	27.50
Business Writing		
____ WBPC	Write Better with a PC	$19.95

☐ Bill the appropriate book prices plus UPS shipping and handling (and sales tax in California) to my ____VISA ____MasterCard:

    Card number_____

    Valid thru (month/year) _____

    Cardowner's signature _____

☐ Bill me.

☐ Bill my company. P.O. #_____

☐ I want to **save** UPS shipping and handling charges. Here's my check or money order for $_____. California residents, please add sales tax to your total. (Offer valid in the U.S.)

* Prices are subject to change. Please call for current prices.
** Available when DOS 6.0 is released

To order more quickly,

Call **toll-free** 1-800-221-5528

(Weekdays, 8 to 5 Pacific Standard Time)

Fax: 1-209-275-9035

Mike Murach & Associates, Inc.

4697 West Jacquelyn Avenue
Fresno, California 93722-6427
(209) 275-3335

fold

fold

BUSINESS REPLY MAIL

FIRST-CLASS MAIL   PERMIT NO. 3063   FRESNO, CA

POSTAGE WILL BE PAID BY ADDRESSEE

Mike Murach & Associates, Inc.

4697 W JACQUELYN AVE
FRESNO CA 93722-9888

NO POSTAGE
NECESSARY
IF MAILED
IN THE
UNITED STATES

fold

fold